UNVEILED
The Twenty & Odd

Documenting the First Africans in
England's America, 1619–1625 and Beyond

Best Wishes –
KIKnight
1619-2019

UNVEILED
The Twenty & Odd

Documenting the First Africans in
England's America, 1619–1625 and Beyond

K. I. Knight

First Freedom Publishing

First Freedom Publishing, LLC
Florida

ISBN 978-1-7338077-0-8

Library of Congress Control Number: 2019903454

Copyright © 2019 by K. I. Knight

www.firstfreedompublishing.com

Book Design by Pro Production Graphic Services
Jacket Design by SJulien.com

Printed in the United States of America

First Edition

*This book is dedicated to the descendants
of the first Africans to arrive in the
English settlement of Virginia in 1619/1620*

Contents

Contents

Acknowledgments

This book would not have been possible without the unwavering love and support of my husband, Thomas Knight, who over the last thirteen years allowed me to dedicate thousands of hours to research—at times a muse, but ultimately, a catalyst in the quest for the truth about the first Africans who arrived in 1619 and 1620, one of them his ancestor.

I am grateful for those who have guided me along the way: whether a fellow descendant, author, historian, genealogist, librarian, community organizer, or truth seeker, your appearance during this journey was pertinent. From sparking the smallest of clues to triggering the largest of realizations, all of you were necessary to put the pieces of the puzzle back together. The truth is a story buried deep, veiled under turmoil and deceit with the many variable parts assembled four hundred years ago to hoodwink the councils and courts and allow a powerful earl to retain his head.

Acknowledgments

On my production team, I want to thank:

To my editor extraordinaire, Bob Land (www.boblandedits.blog spot.com); my superb graphic designer, Rosanne Schloss (www .proproductiongs.com); the late artist, Richard C. Moore (www.ship -paintings.com), and Sharon Julien (www.sjulien.com), my national award–winning cover artist—a huge thank-you. Without you all, this very important history wouldn't be seen with such bright light.

And last, but certainly not least, to the descendants of the "twenty and odd"—I hope and pray a new light of truth will shine down upon us all, allowing the first Africans of 1619–1620 to take their true place in history.

Preface

For four hundred years the first Africans brought to the young English settlement of Virginia in 1619 have remained somewhat of a mystery. A scandalous event, and their entanglement in the ensuing cover-up, shrouded the first Africans—robbing them of their place in history. We now know that the plot to whitewash the event was a grander scheme than previously realized. In today's society, with the World Wide Web connecting historical archives around the globe, a new look at the Africans' footsteps reveals their true circumstances. We can now piece together the puzzle revealing who they were and the lives they led.

This work does not reexplore the highly documented work of historians Linda Heywood and John Thornton, which fully describes the circumstances surrounding the Portuguese war on the ancient western kingdoms of Africa in the sixteenth and seventeenth centuries. This work concentrates on detailing the path the first Africans traveled from their homeland in Africa and how they lived, thrived, loved, and died, along with the vital contributions they made to the survival of the small settlement of Virginia, which eventually became the first English colony in North America. The truth about the first Africans will no longer be shrouded under a narrative controlled by and riven with the deadly sins of power, greed, and envy.

The vast array of participants involved in facilitating their arrival, whether aware or not, demonstrated a worldly command of their actions, each a special cog in the wheel of the global evolution of North America. An enmeshed international trail, touching the regions of Japan, Spain, Portugal, Angola, Jamaica, Mexico, and England, all led to the small settlement of Virginia. In the first fifteen years of the struggling English settlement's existence, thousands of immigrants from England lived and died in Virginia's harsh conditions. When the Africans arrived at the mouth of the Chesapeake Bay at Point Comfort in August 1619, their vision of Virginia must have been nothing short of pure panic. From their international iron-trading kingdom in Africa they found themselves in the depths of Virginia's untamed wilds.

The Africans' arrival was a twist of fate that brought down upon the Virginia Company (the Company) an intense round of criminal accusations and political wrangling. Yet if the Africans hadn't arrived, the struggling settlement of Virginia may have been a total failure. Fortunately for Virginia, with the Africans came their knowledge. From their homeland they spoke several languages, including European ones, and knew how to barter and trade, raise livestock, and grow crops—tobacco as well as essential foods necessary to maintain some type of existence, which ultimately allowed Virginia to mature from a starving settlement into a somewhat manageable venture. Their influence on the English plantation was undeniable, and the Africans became indispensable.

Preface

In 1618 Virginia had become a known pirates' haven, where the raw, primitive conditions forced the starving settlers to become accepting of any and all plunder or substance brought to the shores of the James River. Remarkably, the power behind the settlement's continual pirating progression was Robert Rich, who would inherit the Warwick earldom from his father. Rich's vast inheritance would make him the most influential investor in the New World, with deep pockets and a fleet of ships that rivaled the king of England's. The Rich ships were commonly leased for Company matters, with a continual triangular route from England to Bermuda to Virginia and back.

In addition to his extensive fleet, Warwick co-owned the *Treasurer*, a man-of-war, with Samuel Argall, which they commonly used as a privateer in the Indies. In 1617 Argall had been left in control of Virginia when Honorary Governor West returned to England. Under Argall's governorship of Virginia, the privateering ventures of the *Treasurer* thrived. Argall was an ample partner to Warwick, commonly turning his head as the *Treasurer* came and went, preying upon the Spanish Catholics who traveled through the Indies in their galleons.

In late 1618 in London, Edwin Sandys was elected as treasurer of the Virginia Company, and George Yeardley became the newest governor of Virginia. Neither had any idea what they were stepping into. Before sailing for Virginia and officially taking his seat in Virginia as governor, Yeardley was knighted by King James I. Simultaneously, Edwin Sandys received the record books from the Company's previous treasurer, Sir Thomas Smythe. Unbeknownst to most, the Company was drowning in a tide of debt. Sandys, an investor and a politician who sat in the House of Commons, was determined to change the Company's trajectory. With Sandys delving deep into the Company's enterprise, Warwick's pirating activities took center stage. Sandys felt that

Warwick's bootlegging activities while under King James's treaty of peace with Spain were simply too dangerous for the Virginia Company's viability. The piracy had to stop.

To the detriment of his own future, Sandys pressed heavily on the powerful Earl of Warwick to halt his risky side venture. Sandys's demands fell on deaf ears until Warwick and his associates overplayed their hand and a great scandal erupted. Sandys moved to check Warwick, and an unlikely game of pursuit ensued.

The move divided the investors of the Virginia Company into two factions: one with the Earl of Warwick and one against.

In the spring of 1618 the *Neptune* sailed from England carrying Thomas West to Virginia. West was the twelfth Baron De La Warr, who had served as an earlier governor in Virginia, as well as being a business partner of the Earl of Warwick's. West was returning to the Virginia governorship and carried the Privy Council's orders for the acting governor, Samuel Argall, to return to England for questioning of alleged illegalities.

Following the *Neptune*'s departure to Virginia, Warwick ordered the *Treasurer* to sail ahead and warn his partner, Samuel Argall, of the coming orders. En route, the *Treasurer* met the *Neptune*, and Elfrith, the *Treasurer*'s captain, came aboard. After sharing food and drink, the two ships parted and sailed on to Virginia, unalarmed. The *Treasurer* arrived just days before the *Neptune* and seemingly advised Argall of Lord De La Warr's pending arrival.

When the *Neptune* arrived in Virginia, Lord De La Warr was found dead, and his pilot, Edward Brewster, was making accusations against the *Treasurer*'s men. Upon confirming Lord De La Warr's orders from England, an angry Governor Argall ordered the

Treasurer to be refit with the contents and crew of the *Neptune*. After its refitting and under the cover of a fishing venture, Argall gave his *Treasurer* orders to sail to the Indies in search of loot to plunder. At the same time, Argall sailed for Bermuda, where Rich's allies helped Argall in constructing a story to support Warwick's. Undoubtedly, if Argall were to go down for pirating, Warwick would have been at risk too. Once Argall had his story straight, he sailed to England to face the council.

Then, in the latter part of August 1619, with the arrival of an English privateer carrying a Dutch marque, the first Africans were brought to the shores of Point Comfort. The ship's captain, John Jope, told a story of a Spanish piracy and named the *Treasurer* as his accomplice. A few days later, the captain's story quickly became undeniable when the *Treasurer* sailed into Point Comfort with a full underbelly of Africans. The powers that be must have been on high alert. Just weeks earlier, the most recently elected governor, George Yeardley, had received an order from Sandys for the detention of Warwick's *Treasurer*.

Without question, the Africans would have further complicated Warwick's and Argall's legal issues. An English ship pirating a Spanish galleon was no small matter.

1

Massacre on the Kingdom of Ndongo

From the Atlantic Ocean, narrow coastal cliffs ascend over four thousand feet to a vast plateau extending into the central region of Western Africa, where in 1619 the Bantu-speaking Kingdom of Ndongo was located, in modern-day Angola. Across the immense highlands were small livestock-producing villages, and to the eastern interior the Ndongo Kingdom capital of Kabasa—a grand city of artisans, bustling with merchants from near and far selling their commodities in Kabasa's international market, which rivaled the silk and spice markets of the Far East. The Crown's residence, however, was reportedly in or near the thatched-roof city of Pungo nestled at the foot of the Pedras Negras—known as the black rocks of Pungo.[1] Remaining today, the mystical rock formations stand 350 feet high above the African savannah and provided the Crown's guard additional protection as well as a viewing platform to protect against raids and intrusion, an uncommon safeguard.[2] Late in the fifteenth century

King Alfonzo I of Ndongo had allowed the Portuguese Jesuits to enter his kingdom and educate his people in the ways of Catholicism, and the kingdom became Catholic. Over one hundred years later, in the early seventeenth century, their Catholic given names offer proof.[3]

The Kingdom of Ndongo had endured drastic change. The new leadership was young and inexperienced, making the time ripe for a swift capture by the ever-looming Portuguese Army. Crowned only two years earlier in 1617, the young king Ngola Mbandi hadn't acquired the support of the local *sobas* (rulers) and was in the sights of the recently appointed Portuguese governor, Manuel Mendez de Vasconcelos. After the annual rains rescinded in early 1619 the Portuguese governor decided the time was right. The governor contracted with the Imbangala to raid the region, enslave the citizens, and seize the kingdom.[4] History would prove King Ngola Mbandi of the Ndongo Kingdom to be an easy target.

The Imbangala, an African contraband tribe of mercenaries—reportedly cannibals—were feared throughout the land. With jagged teeth that could rip human flesh from the bone, their bodies covered in oils and painted in ash, their visual impact was staggering.[5] When the Imbangala struck the Kingdom of Ndongo, terror reigned throughout, causing the young king to forsake his crown, abandon his many wives and children, and flee.[6]

In the rabid turmoil and without ample leadership, the kingdom fell quickly. Regardless of their status, the people of Ndongo, royals and servants alike, were stripped of their belongings, beaten, and bound. Marched for hundreds of harsh and unforgiving miles by the Imbangala, they trudged to the coastal port of Luanda, where they were delivered to the maritime slave traders.[7] The Ndongo people were contained among others captured in previous Portuguese raids on the Congo region, to the north of Ndongo.[8] Imprisoned and unaware of their fate, the enslaved waited for the next ship to arrive.

Notes

1. Heywood and Thornton, *Central Africans*.

2. Map of the Pedras Negras, City of Pungo, Angola.

3. Heywood, *Njinga*.

4. Heywood and Thornton, *Central Africans*.

5. See https://blackthen.com/imbangala-death-war-culture/; https://www.britannica.com/topic/Imbangala.

6. Heywood and Thornton, *Central Africans*.

7. Ibid.; Sluiter Collection.

8. Heywood and Thornton, *Central Africans*; Sluiter Collection; Thornton, *Cultural History*.

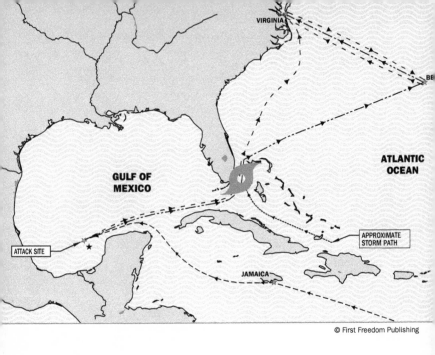
© First Freedom Publishing

KEY

– – – – – – – – – –	SAN JUAN BAUTISTA
– – – – – – – –	TREASURER
–·–·–·–·–·–	WHITE LION

1619

MIDDLE PASSAGE

2

From the Port of Luanda

When the *San Juan Bautista* left Luanda with a full underbelly, Don Manuel Mendez de Acuña had captained the Spanish ship for less than a year. With 350 bound Africans and an ample crew, the Spanish galleon was heavily burdened. The galleon type was not built to carry human cargo, and the quarters were unusually tight. Within no time, much of the *Bautista*'s enslaved were ravaged by the harsh conditions of the journey, and her crew had begun to struggle. Inevitably, filth and dysentery took hold, and sickness soon threatened the *San Juan Bautista*'s entire haul. After sailing nearly fifty-six hundred miles and with the loss of one-third of his cargo, Captain Mendez de Acuña decided he could sail no farther. He made port in Jamaica for medicine and enough supplies to sustain his withered cargo to their destination. The treatment and provisions didn't come cheap as the Spanish captain exchanged twenty-four African boys in trade before setting sail on the final leg of his journey—an additional thirteen hundred miles to the Spanish port of Veracruz, New Spain.[1]

From the Jamaican port the *San Juan Bautista* headed west-northwest. After weeks of travel and within miles of its destination, in the early hours of the morning with a heavy fog lingering beneath the dark rain clouds, the thunder of a cannon was heard. Two English warships fired upon a stagnant Spanish galleon. In 1619 Spain and England were under an agreement of peace, but on the open seas, peace was only an illusion. Away from the Crown's reach, piracy continued to rage between the two countries under the cover of foreign marques.

Under normal circumstances, a Spanish galleon carried adequate defenses to protect the Crown jewels and important documentation it transported to and from the Spanish mainland. A Spanish galleon was high on the list of targets for any privateer, and this galleon, albeit with a full underbelly of enslaved Africans, was ripe for the taking. Roaming the seas for weeks the *Treasurer* and *White Lion* had finally found their prey. The galleon, operating as a slaver, was caught defenseless just miles from its destination of Veracruz. In the summer of 1619, in the Bay of Campeche off the coast of Veracruz, a piracy was committed.[2] Unbeknownst to all involved, this single act of piracy would alter the New World forever.

After the initial assault and with the imminent threat of an overtaking, the Spanish captain quickly surrendered. As the two captains boarded the galleon, Captain Mendez de Acuña quickly declared what remained of the cargo he had purchased in the port of Luanda. In disbelief of his declaration, the privateers took hold of the ship, pushing off the captain and his crew in a pinnace, and descended into the underbelly of the *San Juan Bautista*. Consumed by the gaseous stench, they found nothing more than the enslaved Africans the captain had declared. The two English captains, in need of realizing some type of treasure, chose sixty of the healthiest captives.[3] After ample discussion, the decision was made to sail for Virginia, where they believed they would find safe haven.

As they rounded the coast of Spanish La Florida, the two ships, the *Treasurer* and the *White Lion*, sailed north into rougher seas. From the south came a mighty storm with damaging wind and heavy rains, which firmly challenged the vessels. When the winds subsided and the seas calmed, the *White Lion* had managed to prevail, while the damaged *Treasurer* floundered behind, and one had lost the other. Running from the storm, the *White Lion* had blown off course. With the experience of her pilot, the *White Lion* turned northward, where he knew they would sail upon Bermuda. Remembering the vast reefs from previous voyages, they were able to sail on Somerset at the southwestern tip of Bermuda, where they anchored. Concerned with the dire condition of the famished Africans, the *White Lion*'s captain decided to send four of his crewmen with two of the Africans inland to see if they could find relief. With no word from his crew, each passing hour would have lingered like days. Finally, the word came: the *White Lion*'s crewmen along with the Africans had been detained and the request to enter the harbor denied.[4] Under a fit of rage, the captain reportedly announced that he "would just as soon throw the Africans overboard" than watch them wither. When the *White Lion* left Bermuda under duress, the ship must have met the Englishman Kirby. Kendall reported later he had purchased fourteen Africans from Kirby, who reported he found them "floating upon the seas."[5]

About August 25, 1619, the *White Lion* glided into Point Comfort and dropped anchor. The port commander, William Tucker, climbed aboard, and the English captain Jope declared his cargo under his Dutch marque of Maurice of Nassau, Prince of Orange. Jope proclaimed he fell in consort with the *Treasurer* in the West Indies, with whom he took the poor souls from a faltered Spanish ship in the Bay of Campeche.[6] When Commander Tucker questioned Jope as to the whereabouts of the *Treasurer*, Jope explained how he lost the *Treasurer* in the storm. Because of Jope's Dutch marque he was welcomed into the settlement, and the balance of the Africans were traded to the governor and cape merchant for food.[7]

The *Treasurer* arrived within a few days, and Captain Elfrith found that fate had dealt him a short hand. When he landed at the mouth of the James River, Tucker, Point Comfort's commander, came aboard and Elfrith declared his cargo under the Italian marque of the Duke of Savoy. Tucker advised Elfrith that his Duke of Savoy's marque had expired, and permission from the new governor in Jamestown was necessary to allow him to disembark and sell his cargo. Promptly, the commander, undoubtedly aware of the warrant against the *Treasurer*, sent word to the newly appointed governor Yeardley in Jamestown of the *Treasurer*'s arrival.

Unbeknownst to Captain Elfrith and the *Treasurer*'s owners, with undaunting determination to stifle the pirating in Virginia, Edwin Sandys, the newly elected Virginia Company treasurer, had sent a warrant to the governor. The warrant contained orders to detain the *Treasurer* should the ship return to Virginia.[8] Trying to lure Elfrith upriver to Jamestown, or so it seemed, Governor Yeardley sent two of his men to Point Comfort to escort the *Treasurer* back. Once the governor's men, William Ewens and Lieutenant William Pierce (Peirce), arrived at Point Comfort, they reported back that they only saw her sails as the *Treasurer* disappeared into the Chesapeake.[9] Why did the *Treasurer* flee? Was Elfrith tipped off as to the order for the *Treasurer*'s detention by William Tucker, the port commander? Or was it the realization that his expired marque had turned his privateering expedition into pirating? Regardless, the *Treasurer* sailed from Point Comfort as mysteriously as she had come.

When the *Treasurer* left Virginia, she sailed for Bermuda, where Elfrith believed he might find protection through the *Treasurer*'s owner, the Earl of Warwick. Warwick's deep pockets had allowed for a web of allies looking after his interests, not only in Virginia but in Bermuda as well.[10]

The *White Lion*'s captain Jope and pilot, Marmaduke Rayner, remained in Virginia until after the end of September, when they sailed for England, no doubt stopping in Bermuda to regain his crew and the two Africans,[11] all along with a letter to pass along to the English ambassador Sir Dudley Carleton, from John Pory—Governor Yeardley's personal secretary, who referenced the escapades of the so-called Flemish ship.[12] At the same time the *White Lion* sailed from Virginia, the *Treasurer* was arriving in Bermuda. The *Treasurer* had been seen passing Gurnet Rock, and her condition was noted as very poor.

> we mett with the Treasurer so weather beaten and tourne, as never like to put to sea again, but lay her bones here.[13]

Upon the *Treasurer*'s arrival Captain Daniel Elfrith declared his cargo.

> 29 Negros, 2 Chestes of graine, 2 chests of wax, and a smale quantity of tallow.[14]

The Africans purchased in Luanda and put aboard the *Treasurer* in the Bay of Campeche had now traveled an additional two thousand miles. After more than ten thousand total nautical miles, their condition was very poor at best.

In Virginia, fate had dealt Elfrith's hand; Bermuda would be no different. Bermuda's governor, like Virginia's governor, had changed since Elfrith last anchored. In the early summer of 1619, when Elfrith headed out from Bermuda to roam and pilfer in the West Indies, Governor Daniel Tucker was in command. Called to England to argue a case, Governor Tucker reluctantly left Lieutenant Governor Miles Kendall in charge.

Arriving simultaneously with the *Treasurer* was Tucker's replacement, the newly elected governor, Captain Nathaniel Butler, eager to take over his post. But before Butler could take his seat, Kendall had allowed the *Treasurer* to unload its maritime contraband. However, due to the Duke of Savoy's expired marque, the Africans were placed in the longhouse on the company's public lands until the legalities of the piracy could be worked out.[15] Immediately, Warwick's allies went to work to figure a scheme to protect the *Treasurer* and her owners. With whispers turning to accusations, and in hopes of suppressing the situation, John Dutton, who took the reins of sheriff in Robert Rich's absence, removed the *Treasurer*'s Africans from the public land and placed them at Warwick's estate.[16]

The Africans whom the *Treasurer* brought were not the first Africans in Bermuda. In 1617 at least four African men were living and working in Bermuda: Symon, Fernando, James, and Anthony.[17] Then, in early August 1619, fourteen Africans were said to be brought to Bermuda by Captain Kirby, an Englishman, known to roam the West Indies, pilfering and plundering without commission. When Kirby arrived with the Africans in Bermuda, he reported to Interim Governor Kendall that he had "found them floating on the seas."[18] Kendall then traded Kirby the bulk of the corn on hand from Bermuda's reserves for the fourteen Africans.[19]

When Captain Nathaniel Butler was finally seated as governor and he examined the books, he discovered the purchase of Kirby's fourteen Africans. Governor Butler thought Kendall's transaction with Kirby to be deplorable. Kendall had left the Bermuda settlers with nothing for bread until the next harvest.[20] Butler's disdain for Kendall deepened over the next year when the whispers about Kirby's Africans found their way to the governor's ear, with affirmations "they were taken from a Captain Youppe."[21]

Notes

1. Translation of a piracy complaint by Captain Manuel Mendez de Acuña detailing his cargo (Sluiter Collection); Hashaw, *Birth of Black America*.

2. Original transcription of receipt for slaves purchased in the port of Luanda (Sluiter Collection). Note that the name of the ship is the *San Juan Bautista*, not the Portuguese translation São João Bautista, as many historians refer to it. (See Sluiter, "New Light": "I have changed the ship's and its captain's names to reflect Portuguese orthography rather than the Spanish of the documents.")

3. Original transcription of receipt for slaves purchased in the port of Luanda (Sluiter Collection); Sluiter, "New Light."

4. Manchester Papers, 252 (Rev. Lewes Hughes to Nathaniel Rich, August 12, 1619, telling of four Englishmen and two Negroes castaway in the depths of Somerset [Somers Isles] and believed to be from the *White Lion*).

5. Lefroy, *History*; Ives, *Rich Papers*; Burk, *History*, 326.

6. Rolfe to Sandys, in Kingsbury, *Records*, 3:243.

7. Ibid.

8. Craven, *Dissolution*, 130; Instance and Prize, Libels 80, no. 123, Warrant for the Treasurer, PRO.

9. Rolfe to Sandys, January 1620, in Kingsbury, *Records*, 3:243.

10. Dutton to the Earl of Warwick, January 20, 1620, in Ives, *Rich Papers*.

11. Manchester Papers, 252 ("Two Africans in the depths of Somerset with the crew of the White Lion").

12. Tyler, *Narratives*, 282–87.

13. Dutton to the Earl of Warwick, January 20, 1620, in Ives, *Rich Papers*, 140–42. Dutton sends word to the Earl of Warwick of the arrival of the *Treasurer*, carrying twenty-nine Negroes. Note the specificity of the number regarding the declared cargo.

14. Ibid.; Manchester Papers, 261. The notation in Dutton's letter to Warwick of "29 Negros" is made in both references.

15. Declaring ownership under commission from the Duke of Savoy became a legal matter. The Africans would not be given a specific status, as they were maritime contraband. See Ives, *Rich Papers*.

16. Governor Butler to the Earl of Warwick, October 9, 1620, in Ives, *Rich Papers*, 187–88.

17. 1616–1617 Bermuda census, Bermuda National Library.

18. Miles Kendall to Robert Rich, January 17, 1620, in Ives, *Rich Papers*, 120.

19. Governor Butler to the Earl of Warwick, October 9, 1620, in Ives, *Rich Papers*, 187–88. These fourteen Africans were originally aboard the *San Juan Bautista*, traded or given to Kirby by the *White Lion*'s captain Jope.

20. Butler's charges against Miles Kendall, September 5, 1622, in Ives, *Rich Papers*, 125.

21. Governor Butler to the Earl of Warwick, October 9, 1620, in Ives, *Rich Papers*, 187–88.

3

A Light in Bermuda's Darkness

Within days of the *Treasurer*'s arrival, due to an extralong and difficult transport to Virginia, the *Garland* diverted to Bermuda. With her passengers in need of rest and replenishment before sailing on to Virginia, the *Garland* anchored in the harbor of King's Castle. Nearby was the *Warwick*—a magazine ship owned by her namesake, the Earl of Warwick—leased to the Somers Island Company and waiting for Bermuda's tobacco crop to be loaded and taken back to England. Then, without warning, a great storm approached from the south with hurricane-force winds, and the *Warwick* was driven upon the rocks and lost. After the storm, the magazine ship was an unrecoverable wreck resting at the bottom of the bay. The *Garland,* with some crew aboard during the turbulent winds, had cut her masts to keep from losing the ship and took hold to ride out the storm.[1]

With Bermuda's harvested tobacco crops at stake and no other viable ships available, Governor Butler's only option of transport was to send the *Garland* back to England. After much guarantee and coaxing by the governor's entire council, the newly appointed governor contracted the *Garland*'s captain to take Bermuda's tobacco crops to England. In return, the *Treasurer* would be refit with all the trimmings and fittings to take the *Garland*'s passengers on to Virginia. In the coming weeks, the refitting of the *Treasurer* would prove to be dangerous and risky.[2] In Governor Butler's eyes, the *Treasurer*'s voyage would be twofold and worth the risk. With the *Treasurer*'s most recent assignment, Governor Butler was hopeful he could rid Bermuda of the *Treasurer*'s pirated Africans for Warwick and dispose of the *Treasurer*, alleviating the Spanish piracy issue for Warwick and the Bermuda Company.[3]

At some point in February 1620, the *Bautista* Africans were removed from Warwick's estate and put back aboard the *Treasurer*, sending them back to Virginia along with the *Garland*'s passengers. Butler must have been given secret direction from Warwick's chain of command, as he had no choice; his hands were tied.[4] Butler certainly knew that if the Spanish piracy reached King James's ear, someone would have to pay the price. After all, the previous year Sir Walter Raleigh, once believed to be untouchable, had lost his head for just such a thing. The blame for the piracy needed to lay squarely on the shoulders of the *White Lion*'s captain, Jope, who had no issue with his marque.

Unfortunately for Warwick and Argall, the legal ramifications from the piracy didn't dissipate. Rather quickly, news of the Spanish piracy found its way to Edwin Sandys in England. Whether the information came from the *Garland*'s captain, one of the *Treasurer*'s crew, the sighting of two of the Africans in Somerset with the crew of the *White Lion*, or a letter directly from Virginia wouldn't matter. Sandys had been given what he believed necessary to unseat Warwick and rid the Virginia Company of London from his pirating practices.

Sandys, consumed in his own pleasure, couldn't contain himself. Without the expected courtesy notice usually afforded to an earl and fellow investor, Sandys assembled the Virginia Council, made public the content of Rolfe's letter explaining the events, and declared it his duty to notify the king's council.[5] Simultaneously, Sandys informed Gondomar, the Spanish ambassador, that the Virginia Company of London was in no way involved in the piracy. Sandys believed his efforts were heroic, but in the coming months he was no match for Warwick's power. Sandys's move split the Virginia Company in two. Within months, with the rampant infighting and legal maneuvering, Warwick made the ultimate move and withdrew as an investor, leaving the Company deeper in debt. To cap his move, Warwick quickly developed his own Puritan charter, just north of Virginia in an area he would call New England, and Warwick became the New England Company's principal investor.[6]

Notes

1. Lefroy, *History*, 156.

2. Ibid., 157. This notation suggests that the *Treasurer* was refit for her return to Virginia.

3. Dutton to the Earl of Warwick, January 20, 1620, in Ives, *Rich Papers*, 140–42; Miles Kendall to Robert Rich, January 17, 1620, in Ives, *Rich Papers*, 121–22 (the letter states the Africans Kendall had placed, Butler had removed).

4. Lefroy, *History*, 158.

5. Craven, "Earl of Warwick."

6. The Charter of New England—1620, available at http://avalon .law.yale.edu/17th_century/mass01.asp.

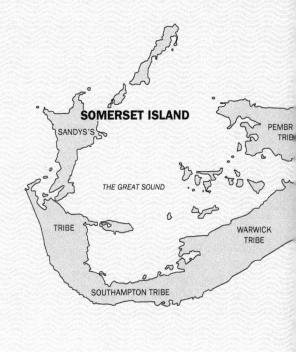

ATLANTIC
OCEAN

SOMERSET ISLAND

SANDYS'S

PEMBR
TRIE

THE GREAT SOUND

TRIBE

WARWICK
TRIBE

SOUTHAMPTON TRIBE

1619

LANDING IN BERMUDA

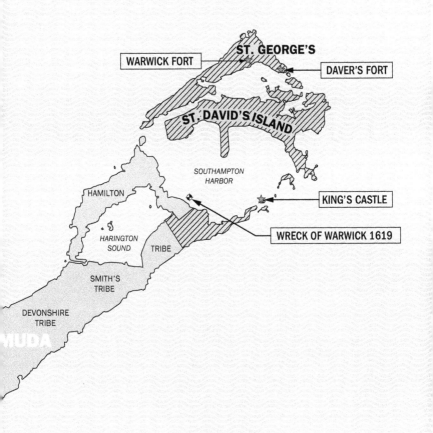

ATLANTIC
OCEAN

KEY

PUBLIC LAND

4

Political Wrangling

When Gondomar confirmed the news of the *San Juan Bautista* piracy through Spanish channels, he was enraged. With the Earl of Warwick in his sights, Gondomar, having the ear of the English king, pushed for legal proceedings. With accusations and unanswered questions, the Virginia Company of London was swirling in controversy and had no choice but to assemble a committee to investigate.

Within months, the notion of an investigation of the stolen Africans reached Virginia and Bermuda, but Warwick's allies had already concocted a scheme to camouflage as many of the details of the "piracy" as possible. When the smokescreen lifted, the overreaching hands were revealed, and there were no options left; the cards were on the table. The Africans would need to be removed from Bermuda. This move would certainly cause questions, and no one would be exempt: Captain Daniel Elfrith;

the *Treasurer*'s crew; Captain Kendall, whom Governor Daniel Tucker left in charge during the summer of 1619; and Governor Nathaniel Butler, who took his seat amid the actual event itself. They all would have questions to answer. Finally, early in 1621 the unsettled matter took a turn and the Privy Council ordered the investigative committee to begin deposing witnesses.

In an odd move, through his own channels, Warwick requested that the governor send a few of the Africans to England. Whether he believed they could assist with testimony about the piracy or if he wanted them for their agriculture abilities was not certain. Regardless, Butler responded by sending three or four of the remaining *Bautista* Africans to England in the summer of 1621.[1] They arrived in the port of Southampton and were escorted to Leez Priory, Warwick's grand estate in Felsted.[2] After weeks of laying the groundwork and with the final rehearsals completed, Antonio was questioned in a preliminary hearing ordered by the Company's investigative council. After taking an oath of truth, Antonio must have had a realization and a change of heart. He told the story of "two ships" pirating the Spanish slaver. He would not falsify his testimony. Warwick knew that if the Privy Council was to hear his account, Warwick's fate would certainly be brought into question. It would be detrimental. In response, Warwick claimed Antonio's baptismal was unverifiable, disqualifying his testimony.

Recognizing that Antonio was a clear witness for his opponent, Warwick quickly removed him from Leez Priory and put him aboard the *James*, sailing for Virginia. By November 1621 Antonio, now with the anglicized name of Anthony, arrived in Virginia and was taken immediately to Bennett's plantation on the south side of the James River.[3] Ultimately, Warwick would need to remove Maria and Juan/John Pedro, the two remaining Africans, as well. Understanding it would be easier to hide them separately, Maria was put aboard the *Margaret and John* and sent to Virginia, with Juan/John Pedro taking a slightly different path. Captain Francis West, another well-connected and trustworthy business partner of Warwick's, was sailing to Plymouth on the *Swan* before continuing on to his plantation in Virginia.

In a stroke of luck for Warwick, Gondomar was called to return to Spain, and with his absence the accusations about the Africans diminished, the investigations turned cold, and the case stalled. But one active court case surrounding the *Treasurer* was still lingering over Warwick's head. Lady Cecily Shirley-West had brought suit against the *Treasurer*'s owners for stealing and defiling her late husband's ship, the *Neptune*. Knowing the undeniable testimony against him, Warwick settled the case, paying a heavy price to Lady Cecily Shirley-West to keep any testimony about the *Treasurer*'s escapades with the Africans out of the High Court of Admiralty.

By 1623 the backbiting had finally reached its pinnacle within the ranks of the Virginia Company. After settling the final case involving the *Treasurer*, the Earl of Warwick still yearned for vengeance against Sandys, who had led the charge against him for two long years. Warwick took one last dig and leaked to the Crown information about the Virginia Company's financial inadequacy. Knowing the records would show the company's finances underwater, Warwick called for an accounting. As he predicted, the Company was unfit. Ultimately, with the infighting among the Company and the insolvency of the venture, King James I withdrew the Virginia Company of London's charter, giving birth to America's first English colony, Virginia.

Notes

1. Governor Butler to the Earl of Warwick, October 9, 1620, stating, "I will quietly deliver them over to your Lordship" (Ives, *Rich Papers*, 188).

2. Hashaw, *Birth of Black America*.

3. *James* manifest, November 1621, available at https://www.pack rat-pro.com/ships/shiplist.htm.

5

The Slaver:
The *San Juan Bautista*

When the *San Juan Bautista* arrived at the port of Luanda on the western coast of Africa, it was already blessed—or possibly cursed. The ship was originally named the *Date Maru*. Commissioned by Date Masamune in 1613, the ship was constructed specifically for Hasekura Tsunenaga's diplomatic mission to New Spain, a mission now known as the historic Keicho Embassy (慶長使節). The *Date Maru* was the embassy's transport and one of Japan's first Western-style, Spanish galleon–type sailing ships.

The Date Maru was completed in forty-five days, with the guidance of several of the Shogun's expert technicians supervising three thousand carpenters, eight hundred shipwrights, and seven hundred smiths. As a part of the mission, the ship would make one of Japan's earliest trans-Pacific voyages. But before setting sail on its first mission, the *Date Maru* was christened the *San Juan Bautista*.[1]

The *San Juan Bautista* set sail for New Spain on October 28, 1613. Aboard with Hasekura Tsunenaga were approximately 180 people, consisting of 10 samurai of the Shogun; 12 samurai from Sendai; 120 Japanese merchants, sailors, and servants; and around 40 Spaniards and Portuguese. Among those last mentioned was a Franciscan friar, Luis Sotelo, fluent in Japanese and traveling as Tsunenaga's interpreter.[2] They arrived with favor at their destination of Acapulco, New Spain, on January 25, 1614. Once Tsunenaga began to discuss the possibility of establishing new shipping routes, the mission met with resistance. With Tsunenaga's options limited, Sotelo convinced Tsunenaga he would be received favorably by the pope, who could possibly lend his approval to sway the Spanish government in favor of Japan's newly proposed shipping routes. When Tsunenaga and the embassy departed Acapulco overland for Veracruz, where a vessel was waiting to take the embassy to the Vatican in Rome, the *San Juan Bautista* returned to Japan on April 28, 1615.[3]

Once at the Vatican, Pope Paul V gave his religious blessing to Tsunenaga's embassy but stopped short of stepping into the commercial dealings of Spanish trade routes. Unfortunately for the embassy, the pope gave his consent contingent upon King Phillipe III's approval. Next, Tsunenaga headed for Madrid. With only a flicker of hope left, the embassy arrived in Madrid, where Tsunenaga met with officials of the Spanish government. Once again, Tsunenaga's words fell on deaf ears, his hopes for establishing new trading routes extinguished. The embassy set sail on their return journey home.

In September 1616, at the request of Luis Sotelo, the *San Juan Bautista* took its second trans-Pacific journey, sailing to Acapulco to retrieve Sotelo, Tsunenaga, and his religious embassy. Upon the *San Juan Bautista*'s arrival in Acapulco the embassy was informed of the negative religious conditions in Japan. Disregarding the undesirable news, Sotelo insisted the *Bautista* set sail for Japan. On the return journey, the *San Juan Bautista* was rerouted to the Philippines, where the interim governor general, Geronimo de Silva, welcomed the ship and identified it as a "well-constructed Japanese vessel." In the summer of 1618, the easily persuaded Tsunenaga sold the *San Juan Bautista* to the acting governor general Geronimo de Silva on behalf of the Spanish government.[4]

When the new Spanish governor general, Alonso Fajardo de Entenza, arrived to take his appointment in July 1618, Geronimo de Silva purchased the *San Juan Bautista* for his own. Eventually, Geronimo de Silva made his way to the Spanish mainland, where he met with King Phillipe III of Spain and presented the Japanese ship as a gift.[5] Grateful, yet indifferent, the king discarded the ship into the political channels of the Spanish government; the *San Juan Bautista* landed in the powerful hands of Count Gondomar, Don Diego Sarmiento de Acuña of the Noble house of Acuña, the ambassador to the English king, James I.[6]

By May 1619 the *San Juan Bautista* had sailed into the port of Luanda, where Acuña's kin, Captain Manuel Mendez de Acuña, had contracted for 350 enslaved African captives.[7]

Notes

1. San Juan Bautista Museum, Ishinomaki, Japan.

2. Pages, *Histoire*, 137–61 (letters [in Latin] of Luis Sotelo).

3. Gonoi, "Hasekura Tsunenaga"; Boxer, *Christian Century*, 313–14.

4. Gonoi, "Hasekura Tsunenaga"; Boxer, *Christian Century*, 313–14.

5. Mathes, "Quarter Century."

6. Blair and Robertson, *Philippine Islands*, 16–17.

7. Receipt for sale of 147 slave pieces by Don Manuel Mendez de Acuña (Sluiter Collection). Some historians suggest that the *San*

Juan Bautista was of Portuguese ownership, but that's incorrect. Engel Sluiter translated the Spanish receipt into Portuguese and notes such in his work (see Sluiter, "New Light"). The English Privy Council's notes into the *San Juan Bautista*'s piracy mention the Spanish ambassador Don Diego Sarmiento de Acuña, conde de Gondomar claiming ownership of the *Bautista* Africans, stating they "were his family's Africans." Don Diego Sarmiento de Acuña was born in La Rioja, Spain, and resided in Galacia, Spain, just north of the Portugal border.

6

Two English Corsairs

When Captain Mendez de Acuña reported the piracy on August 30, 1619, in Veracruz, New Spain, he told of "two English Corsairs."

Treasurer

The English man-of-war *Treasurer* of 180 tons had long been associated with both the Virginia Company and the Somers Isles (Bermuda) Company. Owned by Robert Rich (the Second Earl of Warwick) and Samuel Argall, the *Treasurer* roamed the West Indies fishing for plunder. Captained in the early years by Samuel Argall and later by Daniel Elfrith when Argall became governor of Virginia in 1617, the *Treasurer* seemed plagued by scandal. In 1613 Argall lured Pocahontas, the daughter of the Powhatan king, aboard the ship, and kidnapped her from her home. In 1615 after the marriage of John Rolfe to Pocahontas, they sailed on the *Treasurer* to England, where the Native princess died. Matters were no better when Elfrith took the helm. Twice she sailed upon Virginia with her most questionable missions yet. In 1618 the *Treasurer* crossed the Atlantic to warn Governor Argall of an order to return to England for questioning. When the order eventually arrived in Virginia, the messenger was killed. The second event, more politically destructive to the ship's owners, was the piracy in the Bay of Campeche that led to the arrival of the first Africans in 1619.

White Lion

In the sixteenth and seventeenth centuries, many ships carried the name "White Lion." According to historian Tim Hashaw, Major Hugh Jope's genealogical record shows that a *White Lion* was captained by the Calvinist Reverend John Colyn Jope of Merrifield, who married Mary Glanvill. Hashaw further states that the reverend received the *White Lion* from a member of his congregation, James Enrizo. Enrizo, who captained the ship during the Spanish Armada, had received the *White Lion* from the Lord Admiral Charles Howard afterward.[1]

John Jope, a sea merchant out of the port of Plymouth, Devon, who married Elizabeth Sherwill in 1611, was quite possibly the Captain Jope of interest here. His *White Lion* was not in port in the summer of 1619. Supporting this conclusion is also the discrepancy of the ship's size. Howard's *White Lion* was noted to be 140 tons.[2] The *White Lion* that arrived in Virginia in 1619 and again in 1622 was noted to be 160 tons. Further, outside connections can link the sea merchant John Jope of Plymouth, Devon, to the *White Lion*'s pilot Marmaduke Rayner named in Rolfe's letter.

But without access to the records of Major Hugh Jope, and after a complete review of the records of the ports of Plymouth, Southampton, and Bristol, and the county records of Devon and Cornwall, confusion between the two John Jopes' identities in fact remains.[3]

Calculating the Voyages of the *San Juan Bautista*, the *Treasurer*, and the *White Lion*

Travel Route	Distance (nm)	Average Speed[4] (knots)	Travel Time (days)
San Juan Bautista			
Port of Luanda to Jamaica	5,580	4	58
Jamaica to piracy site	920	4	10
White Lion			
Piracy site to Bermuda	1,650	3	23
Bermuda to Virginia	640	3	9
Treasurer[5]			
Piracy site to Virginia	1,500	1.75	35
Virginia to Bermuda	640	0.9	30

The piracy took place in the Bay of Campeche at the end of July 1619. The *White Lion* arrived in Virginia about August 25. Sailing at an average speed of three to four knots, the *White Lion* could have easily sailed to Bermuda, where fourteen Africans were given or traded to Kirby or the governor. The *White Lion* then continued on to Virginia, landing about August 25. If the *White Lion* would have sailed directly to Virginia, the ship would have arrived at Point Comfort between August 10 and August 13. If the *Treasurer* was damaged in the storm near current-day Miami, for the first seven hundred nautical miles the ships would have sailed at a higher rate of speed. Therefore, from the Bay of Campeche to Miami, sailing at three to four knots per hour, the *Treasurer* would have rounded the tip of La Florida, heading north in about six to eight days.

After receiving terrible damage in the storm, as detailed later in Bermuda, the *Treasurer*'s speed would have significantly decreased from Miami to Virginia. If the *Treasurer* limped along at three-quarters of a knot per hour, the ship would have arrived twenty-nine to thirty-one days after the initial incident in the Bay of Campeche. Using the following calculations, the *Treasurer* would have arrived around August 29 or August 30, approximately four days after the *White Lion* arrived in Virginia on August 25.

Treasurer						
Routes/speed	**5 knots**	**4 knots**	**3 knots**	**2 knots**	**1 knot**	**.75 knots**
Bay of Campeche to Miami (700 nm)	5 days	6–7 days	8–9 days	12–13 days		
Miami to Virginia (475 nm)				8–9 days	17–18 days	23 days
Virginia to Bermuda (625 nm)						30–31 days*

*Leaving Virginia on or about August 29, 1619, and arriving the end of September 1619.

Notes

1. Hashaw, *Birth of Black America*.

2. Corbett, *Drake and the Tudor Navy*, 2:157.

3. Boyd's Marriage Indexes.

4. Assumed average speed of 3 knots (3 nm/hour) for a man-of-war–type sailing ship.

5. Average speeds for the *Treasurer* based on the time it took the ship to sail from Virginia to Bermuda in August/September 1619. The average speed is calculated based on the distance between sites, reflecting the damage the *Treasurer* sustained in the storm.

Battle of the
San Juan Bautista—1619

Maritime Artist: Richard C. Moore;
commissioned by K. I. Knight, 2011

7

Identifying Those Involved

*About the latter end of August, a Dutch man of Warr of the bur-
den of 160 tons arrived at Point-Comfort, the Commander named
Captain Jope, his Pilott for the West Indies, one Mr. Marmaduke,
an Englishman. They mett with the Treasurer in the West Indyes,
and determined to hold consort ship hitherward, but in their passage lost one the other. He brought not anything but exchanged
20, & odd Negars which he traded to the Governor and Cape
Merchant bought for victualle (whereof he was in great need as he
pretended) at the best and easiest rate they could. He had a large
and ample comyssion from his Excellency to range and to take
purchase in the West Indyes.*[1]

This initial report from John Rolfe to Edwin Sandys was
undoubtedly skewed. The author of the above letter, dated
January 1620, undoubtedly knew the event would cause
issue and tried his best to camouflage the participants. At the time

the letter was penned, the web of protection surrounding the Earl of Warwick was already in motion. "20, and odd" was used because Rolfe was unaware of the total number returning on the *Treasurer* in the upcoming weeks.

Captain John Jope (b. ?–1631)

In Rolfe's letter, Jope was named a "Dutch man" who brought the first Africans to the English settlement of Virginia in the latter part of August 1619. This was nothing but camouflage for the English sea merchant and part-time privateer John Jope of Plymouth, Devon. Jope was known to carry a Dutch marque from the prince of Orange. Between the Netherlands, England, Bermuda, Virginia, and New York, he was well traveled and well known. With Jope having friends in every port throughout the English world, John Rolfe could camouflage his identity under this Dutch marque. Jope of Plymouth/Devon continued to captain merchant ships until his untimely death in 1631.[2]

Marmaduke Rayner (ca. 1574–?)

Marmaduke Rayner (Reynor) was noted in Rolfe's letter to Edwin Sandys as "one Mr. Marmaduke" in the West Indies, "an Englishman." This statement was also written as ambiguously as possible.[3] Truth be told, Rayner was well known to several of Virginia's leaders. Marmaduke Rayner, like John Jope, frequented ports throughout the English and Dutch worlds. "A trusted and most fit messenger,"[4] Marmaduke carried a letter written by John Pory, Governor Yeardley's personal secretary in Virginia, and delivered it to the English ambassador to the Netherlands. Another letter ambiguously described the *White Lion* as "a man of warre of Flushing," a ship that carried the Dutch marque of the prince of Orange, falling into consort with the *Treasurer* carrying an expired commission.

Having mett with so fit a messenger as this man of warre of Flushing, I could not but imparte with your lordship . . . these poore fruites of our labours here. . . . The occasion of the ship's coming hither was an accidental consort ship in the West Indies with the Tresurer, an English man of warre also, licensed by a Commission from the Duke of Savoye to take Spaniards as lawfull prize.[5]

Marmaduke Rayner, like John Jope, was a member of St. Andrew's Parish in Plymouth, Devon, where he married Thomasine Loo on October 2, 1593.[6] In March 1620 a committee of the Virginia Company adopted Governor George Yeardley's recommendation to employ Rayner "to explore the surrounding region in a logical manner which would produce good benefit to the Plantation."[7] This employment of exploring "southward to Roanoke" allowed Rayner to disappear from the immediate reaches of the Privy Council, making it impossible for him to be questioned regarding the *San Juan Bautista*'s piracy. Under his contract, Rayner made three surveying voyages, traveling to the boundaries of Virginia and south into Carolina.[8]

With Marmaduke's association with Captain John Jope of the *White Lion*, in 1626 we find on the ship's manifest one John, a Negro, one of the original Africans taken from the *San Juan Bautista*. Near the same time, in July 1626, Marmaduke was commander of the *Temperance*, noted as lying at Cowes, Isle of Wight. This was possibly where Rayner met with his old compadre, Captain John Jope. Plans were hashed out for Jope to transfer his young African study to Marmaduke, who would return him to Virginia with the rest of the *San Juan Bautista* Africans. The following year, Marmaduke mysteriously seized the *Saker* and sailed for Virginia, where he delivered nothing but one African. For some unknown reason, Rayner refused to allow his crew to unload any cargo. Upon petitions by passenger Samuel Sharpe, the Privy Council ordered Saker/Sacar (the owner) to release the passenger's items. Saker's complaint against Rayner was directed to the lower law courts.[9]

Daniel Elfrith (ca. 1585–1641)

Elfrith was a known active privateer in the West Indies as early as 1607, commanding the *Treasurer*. For the next ten years, Elfrith would partake in pirating Spanish ships when he could go unnoticed. In mid-1613, he wouldn't be so lucky. He arrived in Bermuda with a stolen Spanish caravel full of grain. When the grain was removed, black rats hidden in the containers were unleashed upon the island. To Elfrith's shame, the rats would ravage the young English island for years to come, eating and destroying Bermuda's food source and earning Elfrith the nickname of "the Rat." In 1617 the Earl of Warwick secured a foreign marque from the Duke of Savoy, which allowed Elfrith to once again roam the seas looking for Spaniards to plunder.[10] But before the *Treasurer* returned to the Indies, it received a most interesting mission. Elfrith sailed to Virginia under the employ of the Earl of Warwick. His mission was to derail or slow Thomas West's journey and warn Argall of the impending legal questioning he was now subpoenaed to answer in England. Elfrith made the journey, sailing upon West in the *Neptune*, and pushed on ahead to Virginia to warn Argall. Elfrith's actions were certainly questioned, for when the *Neptune* arrived at Jamestown, Thomas West was dead. To make matters worse, the *Neptune* was dismantled, and the ship's crew and cargo were refit aboard the *Treasurer* before Elfrith sailed from Virginia to the West Indies under Samuel Argall's direction.[11] Elfrith roamed the Indies and in the summer of 1619 fell in consort with his old colleague, John Jope.

By 1624 the painstaking legal issues surrounding the *Treasurer*'s actions in 1618 with the *Neptune* and in 1619 with the *San*

Juan Bautista piracy had calmed, and Elfrith openly continued his pirating practice for Warwick. In 1629 Elfrith, still in the Earl of Warwick's employ, discovered New Providence Island in the West Indies. Within months of the discovery—again, under the leadership of the Earl of Warwick—the Providence Island Company was established: another commercial merchandising company, but this one a hotbed for Puritans.

Robert Rich II, Earl of Warwick (1587–1658)

The Earl of Warwick was a complicated character. Born June 5, 1587, in Nottinghamshire, England, Robert Rich was the oldest child of Robert Rich, First Earl of Warwick, and Penelope Devereaux. The Rich family was seeded deep within the English court for several generations. Robert Rich's grandfather, Richard Rich, was counsel to Henry VIII. His mother, Penelope, was the daughter of Walter Devereaux, the First Earl of Essex, and Lattice Knollys—both with bold pedigrees also extending from Henry VIII. In an arrangement her father made, Penelope married Robert Rich. After four children the marriage was failing, and Penelope returned to court life.

As a juvenile, young Robert lived with his mother at court, where she was said to be the most beautiful flaxen in all the land.[12] Therefore, he was quite familiar and comfortable with court life. Soon she found herself in an open relationship with another aristocrat, Lord Mountjoy. Appalled by their audacity and with the Crown's approval, Robert's father granted his mother a divorce. Without question, this open relationship must have played upon young Robert's psyche.

Robert Rich was educated at Cambridge, at the time a center for devout Puritans. In 1603, at the coronation of King James I, Robert Rich was knighted. Now an accomplished gentleman, Robert married Frances Hatton, daughter and heir of Sir

William Newport (Hatton). Newport was the brother of Admiral Christopher Newport, a privateer, ship captain, and adventurer who helped establish the Virginia Company in 1607. From the beginning the Rich family was an intricate part of the colonial ventures taking place in the New World. After his parents' divorce, his father married Frances Wray. Her sister Isabel married John Smythe, son of "Customer" Smythe and elder brother of Thomas Smythe of the Virginia Company.

The inner workings of the Virginia Company were promising for the younger Robert Rich, who became a major figure in Caribbean trade. By 1618 Robert Rich's involvement within the Virginia Company as well as the Somers Isle Company out of Bermuda had grown deeper. Upon his father's death, Robert inherited the Earldom of Warwick. With intricate connections in Virginia and Bermuda, Robert Rich controlled the majority of England's commercial presence in the Americas. Even with the recent beheading of Sir Walter Raleigh for pirating the Spaniards, Robert's privateering expeditions continued, and the Spanish Catholics were his favorite target. Robert ultimately became one of the wealthiest men in all of England.

Edwin Sandys (1561–1629)

The son of Sir Edwin Sandys, the archbishop of York, and his wife, Cecily Wilford, Sandys was born in Worcestershire, England, and was educated at Merchant Taylor's School and Corpus Christi College, Oxford. Over his life, Sandys had four wives. First was Margaret Everleigh of Devonshire, with whom he had one child. His second wife was Anne Southcott, who died early into the marriage. Sandys then married Elizabeth Eastrey, with whom he produced one more child, but then she died. A widower with two small children, Sandys would need to find another wife. Sandys quickly married his fourth wife, Catherine Bulkeley, daughter of

Sir Richard Bulkeley, Knight of Anglesey. With Catherine, Sandys had twelve more children.[13]

As with marriage, Sandys was much practiced in his career. He was first elected to the House of Parliament in 1589. For seven years, beginning in 1593, Sandys traveled abroad, visiting France, Italy, and Germany,[14] where he became affiliated with Fra Paolo Sarpi, who assisted him in preparing his scholarly work, *Europae Speculum; A View or Survey of the State of Religion in the Western Parts of the World.*

Sometime after 1599 with the impending death of Queen Elizabeth, Sandys pledged his support to King James IV of Scotland. Upon King James's accession to the throne, Sandys was knighted by the king at Charterhouse on May 11, 1603.[15]

In 1604 Sandys sat in the first parliament under King James and identified himself as an "assailant of great monopolies." Portraying himself as an advocate for the rights of others, Sandys tried to establish the civic right for a prisoner in England to have legal representation. In 1614 he was elected MP of Rochester and consequently was appointed high sheriff of Kent from 1615 to 1616.[16] All of his career to date was spent seemingly in service to England. Then in 1617 he was chosen to assist Sir Thomas Smythe, the treasurer, in the management of the Virginia Company. In 1619, with the support of the Earl of Warwick, Sandys replaced Smythe as the treasurer in London.

Under Sandys's regime, Governor George Yeardley was sent to Virginia to establish the General Assembly that first convened July 30, 1619—the first representative body in the North American colonies.[17] The Earl of Warwick's patronage was short-lived after Sandys discovered that Warwick was using the struggling English settlement of Virginia as a pirating home base, a port where Warwick's privateers could unload loot to the starving settlers and reoutfit their vessels before returning to sea. With the death of Sir Walter Raleigh

the previous year, and the Spanish ambassador's ongoing p̣
whispers in King James's ear, Edwin Sandys worried that the
could react negatively against the Company. Warwick's auḍacity
triggered Sandys's aggressive retaliation when the *Treasurer*'s
pirating activities against the Spanish caused unwanted attention for
the Company. In May 1619 Sandys issued that an order be sent to
Virginia to hold the *Treasurer*'s captain and crew for questioning.[18]
Issuance of the order caused the Company to divide into two factions, those with Sandys and the others with Warwick.

Sandys's indentured servitude program increased labor in
Virginia, all while promoting indentured servitude to England's
poorest, suggesting a better life in the Virginia settlement. In
1620 Sandys was removed as treasurer but somehow managed to
remain among the higher ranks of the Virginia Company. In 1622,
with the Native uprising in March (the Great Massacre), Sandys's
servitude program had proven to be detrimental, when nearly one-
third of all of Virginia immigrants perished.[19]

Between November 1619 and February 1624, 4,739 immigrants
had arrived in Virginia. During the same time, 4,624 immigrants
in Virginia had died.[20] Edwin Sandys continued to sit in the House
of Parliament through 1626.

Don Diego Sarmiento de Acuña, Count of Gondomar (1567–1626)

Don Diego Sarmiento de Acuña, otherwise known as Gondomar,
was the eldest son of Garcia Sarmiento de Soutomaior, the Lord
of Salvaterra de Mino, and Juana de Acuña, heiress of the noble
house of Acuña.[21] A powerful Spanish diplomat to England from
1613 to 1622, with one short break, Gondomar was connected in
the innermost circle of King James I of England. Gondomar from
an early age collected works of literature. Knowing of the king's
love for books, Gondomar continually fed his appetite, all while

creating a type of peace between the two countries, with an eventual alliance of a Spanish Match—an English prince and a Spanish princess.

Unfortunately for those involved, when the *Treasurer* committed piracy in 1619, under the grandest of coincidences, the Africans pirated from the *San Juan Bautista* belonged to Gondomar's kin. The *Bautista* had passed from King Felipe III through Gondomar's hands and into the grip of Captain Manuel Mendez de Acuña. When Gondomar received the scandalous news from his maternal cousin, he erupted and demanded that the pirated Africans be returned. Falling on the elevated and deaf ear of Warwick, the case's progress stuttered after demands and questions appeared to be swept under a false narrative concocted by the earl and his cronies.

Sir Nathaniel Rich (1585–1636)

Nathaniel Rich was a colonial merchant adventurer and politician in the House of Commons from 1614 to 1629. He was also the first cousin of Robert Rich, Second Earl of Warwick, and his closest counsel. From his earliest years, Nathaniel was groomed to oversee the legal affairs of his cousin Robert Rich, the future Earl of Warwick. This task would prove to be mountainous. Like Warwick, Nathaniel earned his legal education at Emmanuel College, Cambridge, a Puritan hotbed that helped form their radical religious beliefs. Nathaniel had his hands in every transaction into which Robert Rich, Second Earl of Warwick, entered. It was apparent Nathaniel was running interference for Warwick in a "Draft defending" his cousin that Nathaniel penned in 1620.[22]

Lieutenant Governor Samuel Argall (1580–1626)

Samuel Argall was a seafaring adventurer held over from the times of Queen Elizabeth. Baptized December 4, 1580, he was the son of Richard Argall, Esquire of East Sutton, Kent, and Mary

Scott. Richard Argall was a good friend of Sir Robert Dudley, the Earl of Leicester.[24]

Samuel Argall was in Virginia as early as 1609, when he sailed the newest and quickest route from England, directly due west across the vast ocean. Kin to Sir Thomas Smythe and under the command of Governor Thomas Dale, Argall had quickly risen within the ranks of the Virginia Company. By April 1617 Argall was the lieutenant governor of Virginia, left in command by Governor West to maintain the settlement. But for the next two years under Argall's governance, Virginia declined. Argall was accused of disposing of public property, as the settlement had fallen into a state of poverty.[25] In 1618 the Virginia Company of London issued an order for Governor Argall to return to England for questioning regarding the rumors that Jamestown was a pirates' haven. Lord De La Warr was directed to return to Virginia, taking the order to Argall, and retake his seat as governor. Samuel Argall died at sea, where he was buried.

Governor George Yeardley (1587–1627)

Governor George Yeardley arrived in Virginia in the spring of 1619 from England on the *George*, captained by William Ewens. It certainly wasn't Yeardley's maiden voyage; his first to Virginia was much earlier, in 1609, with many more since. Yeardley had served alongside Samuel Argall under Governor Dale's command as early as 1609. He rose to deputy governor in 1616–1617 and finally governor in 1619.

With "sore weather" in the midst of the frozen winter of 1618–1619, on January 19, 1619, the knighted Sir Governor Yeardley boarded the *George* to return to Virginia once more. With Yeardley's knowledge of Virginia from his earlier experiences, he would find this mission different from all the rest. He brought orders from the Company empowering him to implement a set of reforms that came to be known as the Great Charter. The charter would establish a governing body representing the planters and those invested in the plantations along with a headright system securing their patents.[26]

On April 19, 1619, Yeardley arrived in Virginia, accompanied by his wife, Temperance Flowerdew, whom he had married in 1613. Accompanying Mrs. Yeardley was her kin John Pory, who became Governor Yeardley's personal secretary.[27] The Yeardleys' two children would take the same voyage (Elizabeth, b. 1615; Argall, b. 1617). On the *George* traveling with the Yeardleys was Dr. John Pott, along with Dr. Robert Woodson and Sarah, his wife. Dr. Woodson had been contracted as surgeon for the militia in Virginia, along with Dr. John Pott, the newest Jamestown physician. Upon Yeardley's arrival, he patented one thousand acres of land on Mulberry Island, which he named the Stanley Hundred. He also received a patent for a plantation upriver from his Jamestown residence on the south side of the James, which he would subsequently name Flowerdew Plantation.[28] Stanley and Floridew were both names in Temperance Yeardley's immediate lineage. These two plantations would add to the two thousand acres at Wayanoke he received from the Powhatan chief in 1617, making Yeardley Virginia's largest landowner.

During the first months of Yeardley's return and under his most recent commission, the governor established the first governing body in Virginia, a General Assembly, with the first meeting held on July 31, 1619. About the same time, Yeardley regretfully became entangled in Sandys's crusade against Warwick's *Treasurer*. Yeardley was in receipt of an order from Sandys requiring the governor to seize the ship and hold her captain and crew for questioning the next time the *Treasurer* sailed upon Virginia. This order troubled Yeardley, having been an early comrade of Samuel Argall, the ship's co-owner, for nearly a decade. He had even named his first son "Argall."

In the latter part of August 1619, after the arrival of the *White Lion*, Yeardley heard the first additional information about the *Treasurer* since being put on notice. The *White Lion*'s captain told the port commander of the *Treasurer*'s involvement in the taking of the pirated Africans. With the proper documentation, the port commander allowed the ship's captain and crew to unload their cargo. Governor Yeardley traded the *White Lion*'s captain for at least eight Africans and took them upriver to his Floridew Plantation on the south side of the James. During this exchange Yeardley received the news of the *Treasurer*'s involvement in a Spanish piracy. When Warwick's *Treasurer* arrived at Point Comfort in the latter part of August with pirated Africans in her underbelly, the story was confirmed. Fortunately for Yeardley, he wouldn't have to execute the order against the *Treasurer*. Shortly after the *Treasurer* arrived, she disappeared.

Remaining in Virginia, the *White Lion*'s captain and pilot met with the governor and Pory. The conversation must have been lengthy, with several issues to address. Yeardley now knew the *Treasurer* was illegally involved in an English/Spanish piracy; the contraband was in his possession. In order to protect the *Treasurer*'s owners, the *White Lion*'s crew needed to disappear. When the *White Lion* left Virginia, after September 30, Rayner agreed to carry letters for delivery in England and the Netherlands. The next few months, all of Warwick's allies were at work to devise a plan. By January, Yeardley felt the need to make a personal recommendation to the Company to contract Marmaduke Rayner to survey the outer areas of Virginia and south into Carolina. This employment removed Marmaduke from the reaches of the Privy Council so that he could not be questioned.

In 1623 or 1624 the Yeardleys had one more child, a son they named Francis.[29] Also in 1624 the governor sold his Flowerdew Plantation to the cape merchant, Abraham Piersey, and it seems that Yeardley leased six of the eight Africans to Dr. John Woodson and his wife, Sarah, who continued to live at Flowerdew. By the end of 1624, Yeardley had purchased seven acres within the precinct of James City County, neighboring Captain Roger Smith.[30] The Yeardleys took two of their eight Africans with them to James County to be servants at the Jamestown residence. When the Africans left Flowerdew, they would have returned to Yeardley's possession. At this point, Yeardley would have taken them to his property on the Eastern Shore, thirty-seven hundred acres in Accomack County.[31] Yeardley's final mention of the eight Africans was in his last will and testament, where he requests his estate to be sold:

> ... consisting of goods, debts, chattels, servants, negars, cattle, along with any other things of commodity . . .[32]

Abraham Piersey, Cape Merchant (1578–1628)

Abraham Piersey was a member of the Virginia Company of London and the cape merchant for the Virginia settlement in 1619 when the *White Lion* arrived in the latter part of August. Piersey purchased six Africans from the captain of the *White Lion* and took them to his ample plantation, named Piersey's Tolle.[33] By 1620, when Piersey's Tolle was finally patented, he had seven Africans—four men, two women, and one child since born. After Piersey's first wife, Elizabeth Draper, died, he married Frances Greville-West, who became stepmother to his two children: Elizabeth, born in 1609, and Mary, born in 1613.[34]

Compiled after the Native uprising in March 1622 and after the sickness brought by the *Abigail* in December 1622, the List of the Living and Dead dated February 16, 1623, shows five Negroes at Piersey's plantation. A Negro woman with a young child of hers had been sent to Bennett's plantation in 1622–1623 by Piersey as his contribution to the lookout fort project ordered after the Native uprising of 1622.[35] By 1623 Abraham Piersey was one of the wealthiest men in Virginia, when he purchased three thousand acres from Governor Yeardley, including two plantations, Floridew and Weyanoke.[36]

> This was the year that Yeardley sold this plantation as well as his holding across the James at Weyanoke to Captain Abraham Piercey, one of the leading merchants in the Colony. In 1624, the year of the sale, a population of sixty-three (including eleven negroes) had been listed for Flowerdew Hundred with another eighteen having died in the previous twelve months. In the census of 1625, Piercey's Hundred, as the place was now called, had fifty-seven including its seven negroes (four men, two women and one child). The enumeration included twelve houses, three stores, four tobacco houses, and two boats, all of which had been bought, or built, by Piercey. There was a windmill too, and this, the first in the Colony, had been erected for Yeardley, it is said, in 1621. It stood on Windmill Point, earlier known as Tobacco Point.[37]

In 1624–1625, Piersey's original six—now seven—Africans were located at Flowerdew: the two Anthonys, John, William, one unnamed woman, and one woman with a young child.[38]

In 1628–1629, in the last will and testament of Abraham Piersey, again we find the same seven Africans.[39] For five years following Piersey's death, the Africans were removed to Captain Samuel Matthew's plantation. Abraham's widow, Frances, had quickly remarried Captain Matthews after Piersey's death. Unwilling to relinquish one-third of Piersey's wealth as his will called for, Frances refused to disburse her late husband's estate. Consequently, the estate wasn't settled until Frances's death in 1633, when Mary Hill, Abraham Piersey's youngest daughter, filed suit forcing Captain Samuel Matthews to relinquish Piersey's children's inheritance.[40]

Captain William Tucker (1589–ca. 1644)

In July 1619, William Tucker was the newly elected member of the first assembly representing Kecoughtan, otherwise known as Elizabeth City. He was also the commander of Point Comfort, a port and point of command at the mouth of the James River overlooking the Chesapeake Bay. Tucker was present when the first Africans arrived on the *White Lion* in the latter part of August 1619 and, without question, was in charge of determining whether the ship could unload its cargo. When the *White Lion*'s captain reported to Tucker where and how he took the Spanish vessel while sailing in consort with the *Treasurer*, Tucker must have been on high alert, certainly aware of the warrant from Sandys in London for the *Treasurer*'s detention. When the *Treasurer* arrived four days later, Tucker would have already been aware of the *Treasurer*'s participation in pirating the Africans. He must have also known the Italian marque that Elfrith, the *Treasurer*'s captain, carried had become invalid.

Tucker was among those who took a leading role in the fighting arising out of the Native uprising in 1622. Sometime before 1623 he had become a member of the Governor's Council of Virginia when his wife, Mary Thompson, arrived from England. She was the daughter of Robert Thompson and Elizabeth Harsnett of Hertfordshire and older sister of Maurice Thompson, Warwick's trade manager in Virginia with whom Tucker worked closely.[41] By September 1624 Captain Tucker purchased 150 acres within Elizabeth City County. By 1645 Tucker had acquired over 750 acres. After his death, his Virginia properties were left to his oldest son, William, for his "use and pleasure."[42]

Maurice Thomson (1604–1676)

Maurice Thomson (Thompson) arrived in Virginia in 1617. When the Africans arrived in 1619, Maurice Thomson was living in

Kecoughtan, near or with Point Comfort's commander, Captain William Tucker. Thomson was being groomed as the Earl of Warwick's trade manager in Virginia. Most certainly, he would have been among those involved in camouflaging the *Treasurer*'s piracy. If Thomson wasn't aware of the ramifications of the matter, Captain Tucker would have informed him, using the instance as a teaching moment for his young study. Thomson was obviously a quick study on the financial dealings of maritime trade, and he rapidly prospered, acquiring ships and a tobacco plantation and establishing trading links along the eastern coast from Virginia to Maine.[43] Maurice Thomson was listed in Captain William Tucker's will as "his brother" and appointed him as overseer.

Captain William Ewens (ca. 1579–1650)

William Ewens, a worthy sea captain, was one of two men sent to Point Comfort to bring the *Treasurer* and her cargo upriver to Jamestown in late August 1619. Ewens owned the ship *Charles*, which he leased to the Virginia Company of London, and he frequently captained several transport ships for the Company, including the *George* and the *James*, both owned by the Earl of Warwick. In March 1619 the *George* left England carrying several prominent Englishmen and arrived in Virginia on April 19, 1619. Aboard the *George* were the recently appointed governor George Yeardley and Temperance, his wife; John Pory, Temperance's first cousin; along with Dr. John Woodson and his wife, Sarah.

Ewens's connections within the settlement were beyond question. In September 1619 Ewens was granted four hundred acres on the south side of the James River for transporting settlers and headrights. After the Native uprising of 1622, the Henrico area where the East India School was being erected was devastated. With a library of sorts being established, the contents were transferred to Ewens's plantation, which became known as the College

Land. Later land patents show that William Ewens was in possession of at least four of the original 1619 Africans.[44] These Africans were not included in the 1623 List of the Living and Dead or the 1624–1625 census, leading to the conclusion that they were being hidden—most probably returned on the *Treasurer* from Bermuda in early 1620 and tucked away at Warwick's request. As noted, Captain William Ewens did not reside at his Virginia plantation. He made several long visits, yet he maintained his official residence in Kent County, England, with his wife and children.

Captain and James City Lieutenant Governor William Pierce (ca. 1580–1655)

William Pierce was one of two men sent to Point Comfort to escort Elfrith and the *Treasurer* to Jamestown.[45] In 1619 William Pierce had recently become John Rolfe's father-in-law, with Rolfe's third marriage to Pierce's daughter Jane. William Pierce came to Virginia on the *Sea Venture* in 1610, with Sir Thomas Gates on the *Blessing*. He was captain of the guard at Jamestown in 1617. In December 1619 he patented 650 acres at Mulberry Island, to which he removed and had a house there, as shown by a land grant for 2,100 acres in 1643.[46] Therefore, if Angelo/Angela arrived on the *Treasurer* in 1620, she wasn't taken to Jamestown. Pierce was living at Mulberry Island. In 1623, in the List of the Living and Dead, Pierce was listed at Jamestown with Angela. The same year, William Pierce became captain of Governor Wyatt's guard and lieutenant governor of James City.[47] In the 1624–1625 Muster, Angela was listed again with Pierce. Pierce's house, a wooden building at Jamestown, was in 1624 "one of the fairest in all Virginia." At his home, he had a fine garden in which he raised an abundance of figs and other fruit. In 1632 Pierce stood sixth in the Council of Sir John Harvey, and in 1646 "Capt. William Pierce, Esq." was second in standing.[48]

Deputy Governor Miles Kendall (b. ca. 1587)

Miles Kendall was said to be in Bermuda from the settlement's earliest days and rumored to be kin to Edwin Sandys. In early 1619 Captain Daniel Tucker deputized Miles Kendall as the interim governor of the Somers Isles Company (Bermuda). Upon leaving his command, Tucker warned Kendall "to have care of all things and beware not to have too much acquaintance with the *Treasurer*."[49] Therefore, when the *White Lion* arrived telling the story of how she took the Africans from a Spanish slaver in consort with the *Treasurer,* explanations were forthcoming of her great need for water and food. When four of the *White Lion*'s crew were found at Somerset, they were detained, and again Kendall denied the *White Lion*'s entry into the bay.[50] Within days, Kendall did accept fourteen Africans from a Captain Kirby, who stated he had found them floating on the seas. When the newly appointed governor, Captain Nathaniel Butler, was seated and discovered how Kendall paid for the Africans, he removed them from Kendall's possession, claiming they were the settlement's Africans. By January 1620 Kendall had returned to England and filed a complaint in the courts, demanding his fourteen Africans. Warwick's allies joined forces, making Kendall appear as a no-good, irresponsible excuse for a man. Infighting over the Africans continued even after the case was settled in 1622 and Kendall was awarded a portion of the Africans.[51] In the end, Kendall never received the first African.

Reverend Richard Buck (1580–1624)

Historical records show the details of Richard Buck's 1619 patent on five hundred acres of land at Neck-of-Land, bounded by Mill Creek on the east, Back River on the south, and Powhatan Creek on the west. It is doubtful that Reverend Buck himself lived at Neck-of-Land, instead residing at Jamestown. In 1622, during the Native uprising, Reverend Buck was killed.[52] After his death,

Richard Kingsmill became the caretaker of Buck's children and executor for Buck's property in the Neck of the Woods, one mile north of Jamestown, eventually known as Kingsmill. In the 1623 List of the Living and Dead and in the 1624–1625 census at the Neck of the Woods appears Edward, a Negro man. Most likely, Edward remained with Kingsmill until 1635.

Richard Kingsmill (bef. 1594–aft. 1634)

In 1619 Richard Kingsmill was among the first Virginia Company members to receive grants of land in what was later to become Kingsmill. Richard Kingsmill, a member of the General Assembly, expanded his holdings to 750 acres. He and his wife, Jane, had three children: a son named Nathaniel and two daughters, Susan and Elizabeth. It appears Elizabeth was the only descendant to have offspring.[53] With the Kingsmills having young children, the Buck children would be well placed.

Edward Bennett (1577–1664)

Edward Bennett was a very wealthy and successful English merchant and a Puritan.[54] He was among the Virginia Company's largest investors and closely affiliated with Robert Rich, the Earl of Warwick, as a fellow Puritan leader. In 1621 Bennett was the Company auditor and on several of the Company's committees. Believing he could transport 150 to 200 settlers, in November 1621 Edward Bennett patented 1,000 acres on the south side of the James River overlooking Burwell Bay in the area known as Warrasquarake.[55] In late 1621 Bennett sent his brother Richard and his son Robert ahead to Virginia to start the beginnings of the plantation. By February 1622 the *Sea Flower* had arrived with the first settlers. Not a month later, when building had just begun, on March 22, 1622, the Native uprising stifled the plantation in its infancy. The attack was in response to overexpansion south of the James into the Natives' land. Suffocated by death, Bennett's plantation was abandoned, with the few survivors relocated to Jamestown. After several months and numerous requests by Bennett to resettle the plantation, permission was finally granted in response to Bennett's letter dated October 7, 1622.[56] However, resettlement only came after an agreement was made to build a lookout fort adjacent to Bennett's property. The lookout was to give the settlers advance warning of future attacks with an over-look of Burwell Bay and the mouth of the James River, and out into the Chesapeake.[57]

Edward Bennett personally never set foot in Virginia. After the Native uprising of 1622 Bennett's plantation was abandoned; before the year was up, Bennett's plantation had been reoccupied and changed its name to Bennett's Welcome. When the List of the Living was taken in February 1623, four Africans are listed at Bennett's Welcome: Anthony, Margaret, Frances, and Peter.

Samuel Matthews (1580–1657)

Samuel Matthews (Mathews) arrived in Virginia prior to 1619. By 1621 he was a member of the Governor's Council and a bur-gess representing the stretch up against James City County on the College Land. In 1622 during the Native uprising, Matthews was in England, where he would remain until December 1622, when he returned to Virginia on the *Southampton*. About 1625 Captain Samuel Matthews moved his seat from the south side of the James River to a location near Blount Point at the mouth of the Warwick River and across from Mulberry Island, later called "Denbigh." Matthews's landholdings were vast; in addition to Denbigh, he held land at Henricus and Old Point Comfort. In 1628 his assets grew with his marriage to one of the wealthiest women in Virginia, Abraham Piersey's widow, Frances. In 1629 Matthews was commissioned to rebuild a fort at Point Comfort, which he completed by 1630 when he was paid for his service with an authorization to "have sole trade in the Bay for a year." By 1633 Matthews had lost his wife, Frances, when the co-heirs of Abraham Piersey's estate charged Matthews with concealing portions of their father's wealth. Matthews continued to sit on the Governor's Council, and in 1635 he was involved in removing John Harvey from the governorship. Unfortunately for Matthews, Harvey would remain in control until 1637 and marry his widow's stepdaughter Elizabeth Piersey. During this time Matthews participated in the "second ousting" of Governor Harvey. With a large plantation, Matthews added many Africans after the initial Africans from 1619 were removed from his possession.

Captain Francis Pott (1590–1658)

Francis Pott, the younger brother of Jamestown's Dr. John Pott, was in the Virginia settlement as early as 1629. In 1634 Pott received a commission "for Command of ye fort at Pt. Comfort."[58] By 1635 Pott was a major player in Virginia politics, along with Captain Samuel Matthews and a few others, who were responsible for the initial ousting of the overbearing Governor Harvey.[59] After Pott's commander appointment was terminated for his misdemeanor actions in the governor's ousting, he moved to Northampton County, where he held two separate land grants of two thousand and fifteen hundred acres in Matchepungo.[60] In 1642 he had inherited five hundred acres of land from his brother and quickly sold it to Richard Brewster. Pott recorded an affidavit in 1645 noting the two Driggers children, Elizabeth and Jane, who were indentured to him by their adoptive parents, and Pott's servants Emmanuel and Frances Driggers. At the same time, Pott recorded the brand of Driggers, naming a cow and a calf in his possession. Captain Francis Pott died prior to 1658, when his last will and testament was proven, noting Governor George Yeardley's son, Argall Yeardley, as Pott's godson.[61]

Captain Francis West (1586–1634)

Francis West was the son of the Second Lord De La Warr and brother to Thomas, the Third Lord De La Warr, and John West. All three of the brothers had holdings in the Virginia Company and were undoubtedly within Warwick's group of allies. Early in Virginia's infancy, Francis West was a major contributor to the Company. By the latter part of 1610 Francis West had become the commander of Jamestown, a position he held for many years. In November 1622, while in England and after testifying on behalf of the Earl of Warwick, West was commissioned admiral of New England before boarding the *Swan* and sailing to the New England region, stopping in Plymouth and Weymouth. Noted on the *Swan*'s manifest was John Pedro, a Negro whom West smuggled from Warwick's estate in Felsted and out of England. His appointment as admiral must have been short-lived, because Francis West was back in Virginia by 1624.

From 1619 to 1633 he maintained a seat on the Governor's Council, all while remaining loyal to Warwick through Virginia's transition. Captain Francis West was also associated with the African John Pedro for many years.

Warwick's Allies in Bermuda

Robert Rich, the Younger (b. ?–1620)

Nathaniel Rich's younger brother was also named Robert Rich. Nathaniel trained young Robert to oversee and control most of the commercial movement coming in and out of Bermuda, where he spent most of his time keeping Warwick's privateering under wraps. At the time of the *Treasurer*'s arrival with the Africans in 1619, the younger Robert Rich was yet to return to Bermuda from England with his new bride, Elizabeth Dutton. By the time the young Robert Rich came back to Bermuda in early 1620, he found he had a rather large problem to address. Rich the younger's hands would certainly have been involved in the plot to camouflage the Africans, right up until his untimely death in the fall of 1620.[62]

Governor Nathaniel Butler

Butler arrived in Bermuda simultaneously with the *Treasurer* in September–October 1619. The governor, loyal to Warwick, was instrumental in the removal of Africans from Bermuda. In late 1619 John Dutton and Governor Butler were communicating with Warwick's allies in Virginia and Nathaniel Rich in England to concoct a plan to shroud the pirated Africans the *Treasurer* had brought to Bermuda.[63] The recommissioning and refitting of the fallen *Treasurer* to take the *Garland*'s passengers on to Virginia clearly offered an avenue for the Africans to return to Virginia.[64]

In 1620–1621 Butler again assisted Warwick with sending Africans to England, and in return Butler received a share of land, no doubt as a gift for his services.

John Dutton

In 1619 John Dutton became the younger Robert Rich's brother-in-law. Dutton arrived in Bermuda while Robert Rich was still in England, preparing to return to Bermuda with his new bride, Elizabeth Dutton Rich. Dutton arrived on the *Warwick* in late September 1619 and observed the *Treasurer* at Gurnet Rock.[65] Also on the *Warwick* was the newly elected governor, Nathaniel Butler. When Dutton arrived in Bermuda, he took the self-appointed position of bailiff.

Notes

1. Rolfe to Sandys, January 1620, in Kingsbury, *Records*, 3:243.

2. John Jope's last will and testament, filed in 1631, Devon County Records. See also the afterword to this volume.

3. Rolfe to Sandys, January 1620, in Kingsbury, *Records*, 3:243.

4. Ibid.

5. Ibid.

6. St. Andrew's Parish records, Devon County Records.

7. Neill, *Virginia Company of London*; "Marmaduke Rayner."

8. "Marmaduke Rayner."

9. "William Ewens vs. the Saker," in Coldham, *English Adventurers and Immigrants*, 19; "Virginia in 1626–27."

10. Ives, *Rich Papers;* Lefroy, *History*.

11. *Lady Cecily Shirley-West v. Robert Rich, Second Earl of Warwick* (High Admiralty court case, PRO).

12. Admired by Philip Sidney, who took her for his muse in his sonnet cycle *Astrophil and Stella*.

13. Available at http://www.geocities.ws/madelinefelkins/WillifordWilford.htm.

14. Ibid.

15. Ibid.; *Encyclopedia Brittanica*, s.v. "Sandys, Sir Edwin."

16. *Encyclopedia Brittanica*, s.v. "Sandys, Sir Edwin."

17. Ibid.

18. Kingsbury, *Records*, vol. 3.

19. Ibid.; List of the Living and Dead, dated February 16, 1623.

20. Quisenberry, "First Pioneer Families."

21. Bartolomé, *Don Diego Sarmiento de Acuña, conde de Gondomar*.

22. Ives, *Rich Papers*, 148–54.

23. Ives, *Rich Papers*, 15.

24. Hasler, *History of Parliament*.

25. Fiske, *Historical Writings*, 1:63.

26. "A headright is a legal grant of land to settlers. Headrights are most notable for their role in the expansion of the thirteen British colonies in North America; the Virginia Company of London gave headrights to settlers, and the Plymouth Company followed suit. . . . By giving the land to the landowning masters the indentured servants had little or no chance to procure their own land. This kept many

colonials poor and led to anger between the poor slaves and wealthy landowners" (Wikipedia, s.v. "headright").

27. *George* manifest, available at https://www.packrat-pro.com /ships/shiplist.htm.

28. Ibid.; McCartney, *Virginia Immigrants and Adventurers*.

29. "Temperance Flowerdew."

30. Nugent, *Cavaliers and Planters*.

31. Ibid., 96. "On 6 Sep 1638, re-patented 3700 acres in Accomack County," the patent reciting that the land had been granted to "Sir George Yeardley, Kt., father to said Argoll . . . by order of the Court, 9 May 1623."

32. Yeardley's last will and testament, Colonial Papers.

33. Hatch, *First Seventeen Years*, 66–67.

34. McCartney, *Virginia Immigrants and Adventurers*, 42.

35. Ballagh, "Institutional Origin of Slavery." There is nothing to suggest that a single transfer of possession had taken place after being fixed, though in several cases the Negroes were moved from one place or plantation to another by their possessors. Peter and Frances—child and mother—for example, were transferred from Warrasquarake back to Piersey's Hundred in 1623.

36. Ibid.

37. Hatch, *First Seventeen Years*, 72.

38. Kingsbury, *Records*, vol. 3; 1624–1625 Muster of Virginia.

39. Piersey's last will and testament, Colonial Papers.

40. *Mary Hill v. Mathews*, 1633. Frances died by 1633 when Mary Hill was appointed administratrix of the estate of her father, Abraham Piersey—the executrix, his late wife, having died. Thomas Hill and his wife, Mary, charged Samuel Matthews with having altered the estate of Piersey after his marriage to the widow. The case was dismissed. http:// freepages.genealogy.rootsweb.ancestry.com/~virginiahuddlestons /captain_john_huddleston_of_the_b.htm.

41. https://wc.rootsweb.com/cgi-bin/igm.cgi?op=GET&db= bradsdata&id=I11433.

42. *Gleanings*; St. George and St. George, *Visitation*, 282.

43. *Gleanings*; Quisenberry, "First Pioneer Families," 62.

44. Nugent, *Cavaliers and Pioneers*, 147.

45. Rolfe to the Virginia Company of London, January 1620, in Kingsbury, *Records*, 3:241–48.

46. Nugent, *Cavaliers and Pioneers*.

47. Boddie, *Colonial Surry*, 50 ("A Relation of the Present State of the Colony of Virginia, by Capt. William Perse, an ancient planter of twenty years standing there [prepared in England, 1629]").

48. Wolfe, "William Peirce."

49. Bernhard, *Tale of Two Colonies*, 175.

50. Burk, *History*, 326.

51. Ibid., 326–27.

52. List of the Living and Dead, February 23, 1623.

53. Crozier, *Virginia Heraldica*, 36.

54. McCartney, *Virginia Immigrants and Adventurers*, 125–26.

55. Kingsbury, *Records*, vol. 3.

56. Hatch, *First Seventeen Years*, 87.

57. Boddie, "Edward Bennett"; Morrison, *Brief History*; "Minutes . . . 1622–1624."

58. *The Aspinwall Papers,* Collection of the Massachusetts Historical Society, 132.

59. Fiske, *Historical Writings*, 1:293–99; Neill, *Virginia Carolorum*, 115–31; Virginia Historical Society, "Virginia in 1635."

60. See afterword.

61. Ibid. See also *Virginia Magazine of History and Biography* 1 (December 1893): 198.

62. Ives, *Rich Papers*, 15.

63. Ives, *Rich Papers*.

64. Lefroy, *History*.

65. Dutton to the Earl of Warwick, January 20, 1620, in Ives, *Rich Papers*, 141–42.

8

Dissecting the Original Count

Enter on the credit side the receipt of 8,657.875 pesos by Manuel Mendez de Acuña, master of the Ship San Juan Bautista, on 147 slave pieces brought by him into the said port on August 30, 1619 ... on the voyage inbound, Mendez de Acuña was robbed at sea off the coast of Campeche by English (war ships). Out of 350 slaves, large and small, he loaded in said Luanda, he was left with only 147.[1]

When the *San Juan Bautista* left the port of Luanda, she carried 350 slaves en route to Veracruz, New Spain. The following accounting shows what happened to these people after they were taken from Africa.

Africans on the *San Juan Bautista*, purchased at the port of Luanda		**350**
Deaths en route from sickness	119	
Young boys traded in Jamaica for medicine	24	

Total arrivals in Veracruz[2]	147
Pirated by two English corsairs	60

Like every Middle Passage afterward, the *San Juan Bautista*'s crossing was harsh and inhumane, losing more than half of those aboard—who were bound and enslaved. Records account for 59 of the original 60 Africans taken from the *San Juan Bautista*:

Africans from the *San Juan Bautista*, placed on English corsairs		60
White Lion		30
"Found floating on the seas": traded in Bermuda, August 1619	14	
Brought to Point Comfort (8 to Yeardley, 6 to Piersey)	14	
With the crew of the *White Lion* in the "depths of Somerset"	2	
Treasurer		30
Arriving from Bermuda[3]	29	
Probable death during passage	1	

The "20, and odd" declared in Rolfe's letter was intentionally ambiguous, intended to camouflage the *Treasurer*'s impending return. During the four and a half months it took for Rolfe to write the letter announcing the Africans' arrival, a plan among Warwick's allies had already been devised to shroud and deflect attraction from the scandalous event. In February 1620, of the twenty-nine Africans the *Treasurer* brought to Bermuda, Dutton and Butler shipped as many of the Africans as possible back to Virginia. Later evidence shows that Butler kept the fourteen *Bautista* Africans Kirby had brought to Bermuda and some additional Africans he had already loaned out.[4] When the *Treasurer* returned to

Virginia in early 1620, there were seventeen or eighteen Africans aboard. Immediately they would have been distributed among those most prominent in the Virginia settlement, all of whom had ties to the Earl of Warwick. In March 1620 there were thirty-two Africans in Virginia, seventeen women and fifteen men.[5]

Women arriving on the *Treasurer*	10
Women arriving on the *White Lion*	7
Men arriving on the *Treasurer*	8
Men arriving on the *White Lion*	7
Total Africans in 1620 Census of Virginia	32

Notes

1. Sluiter, "New Light," 397.

2. Ibid.

3. Ives, *Rich Papers*, 141.

4. Governor Butler to the Earl of Warwick, October 9, 1620, in Ives, *Rich Papers*, 185–88.

5. March 1620 census contained in Ferrar Papers, microfilm reel 1, MS 1597A, document 159. See also Thorndale, "Virginia Census of 1619."

9

The Native
Uprising of 1622

I n 1620 Sandys began his continual push to populate
Virginia with a frequent influx of new settlers from
England, expanding growth on the south side of the James
into the Natives' croplands. Many of the surviving settlers were
new arrivals from England. The Virginia Company's treasurer
had pressed hard to populate the settlement through his headright
system, in hopes of seeing profits. Most were not volunteers, but
sent from the reformatories and the streets of England to pay their
legal debt. They were men, women, and children with little famil-
iarity of the survival skills necessary to endure the rabid lands of
Virginia.

By 1622 the Natives had planned a great attack on the settlement
to stifle its growth and reclaim their land. Chief Opechancanough,
the younger brother of the deceased chief Powhatan, attacked the

settlement in a joint raid with the neighboring tribes in hopes of pushing the settlers back across the James River. The attack was impressive; they maimed and slaughtered men, women, and children alike, burned planted crops, and raided livestock. On March 22, 1622, three hundred and forty-seven Virginia settlers died, with an uncertain number of people stolen to be enslaved by the wrathful Natives. Of eighty plantations in Virginia, the surviving settlers pulled their defenses together, abandoned the outlying areas, and made preparations for guarding the eight most viable plantations.

- Jamestown
- College Land
- Elizabeth City
- Marie's Mount (Newport News)
- Flowerdew Plantation
- West & Shirley Plantation
- Southampton Hundred
- Jordan's Journey

Of the eight plantations, Flowerdew was the largest, at one thousand–plus acres, a few miles upriver from Jamestown in Charles City. After the massacre, Abraham Piersey moved his Africans across the river to Flowerdew Plantation as reflected in the List of the Living, which shows fourteen Africans listed at Flowerdew. Because of the lack of damage after the Native uprising, Flowerdew would have been looked to for food replenishment when shortages became an issue within months in the more heavily populated areas like Jamestown and Marie's Mount.

The Africans' knowledge of growing crops and raising livestock provided the settlement with enough food to keep Virginia alive until it could be determined that the outlying plantations were safe for the settlers to return. Attacks on the settlement continued until May 22, 1623, when the settlers devised a plan of trickery to retaliate, poisoning the Natives under the pretense of a parley. The plan worked, and the Native attacks subsided.

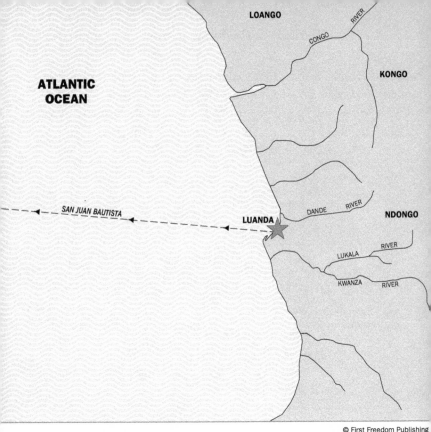

ATLANTIC
OCEAN

LOANGO

CONGO RIVER

KONGO

SAN JUAN BAUTISTA

DANDE RIVER

LUANDA

NDONGO

LUKALA RIVER

KWANZA RIVER

© First Freedom Publishing

AREA OF
INTEREST

1619

FROM THEIR HOMELAND IN AFRICA

— 10 —

The Africans

About the latter end of August, a Dutch man of Warr of the bur-
den of 160 tons arrived at Point-Comfort, the Commander named
Captain Jope, his Pilott for the West Indies, one Mr. Marmaduke,
an Englishman. They mett with the Treasurer in the West Indyes,
and determined to hold consort ship hitherward, but in their pas-
sage lost one the other. He brought not anything but 20, and odd
Negars, which the Governor and Cape Merchant bought for vict-
ualle (whereof he was in great need as he pretended) at the best
and easiest rate they could. He had a large and ample comys-
sion from his Excellency to range and to take purchase in the West
Indyes.

This correspondence is the first to note the first Africans' arrival in the English settlement of Virginia. Dated January
1620, over four months after the event took place, John
Rolfe of Virginia wrote an ambiguous letter to Edwin Sandys,

treasurer of the Virginia Company of London. The words were chosen carefully, with lack of specificity the intent. A "Dutch man of warr," "20, and odd Negars," "one 'Mr. Marmaduke'"—all the phrases presented pertinent information, but with no implication of what the *Treasurer*'s cargo might mean in the short or long run.

Two months later, a census was taken that reflected thirty-two Africans, of whom seventeen were women and fifteen were men. These numbers confirm that the *Treasurer* did indeed return before March 1620, bringing the additional *San Juan Bautista* Africans from Bermuda to be hidden away in Virginia. It would be three years later before another listing of Virginia inhabitants was made. In the List of the Living and Dead dated February 16, 1623, compiled after the Native uprising and after the epidemic brought by the *Abigail* in late 1622, the first mention appears of the Africans' names and locations. The next year the General Muster of 1624–1625 was recorded.

Records of the Africans for the next four to five years are nonexistent, until the deaths of Governor Yeardley and Abraham Piersey in 1628. The eight Africans listed in the employ of Governor Yeardley and the seven listed at Piersey's hadn't changed. Until this time, very little relocation took place for the Africans.

According to Yeardley's last will and testament, the eight unnamed Africans along with all of Yeardley's belongings were to be sold, and for a time the Africans somewhat disappear from the record again. In 1635 they seemingly reappear, exactly seven years after the order to sell the Africans is given. Three to seven years was the common length of a contract of servitude. By 1635 and 1636, Africans began to appear as headrights themselves in several land patents—presumably the eight Africans in Yeardley's will.

The Africans at Abraham Piersey's plantation, on the other hand, are somewhat trackable. Due to the unresolved distribution of Piersey's estate, the seven Africans were removed from Piersey's plantation to Samuel Matthews's plantation. Very soon after Abraham Piersey's death, Piersey's widow married Captain Samuel Matthews and took the Africans—two Anthonys, John, William, Frances, Peter, and an unnamed African woman—with her to Matthews's plantation, where they would remain until Frances Piersey Matthews's death in 1633. With the estate of Abraham Piersey still unsettled, Mary Piersey Hill—along with her sister, Elizabeth Piersey-Stephens—petitioned the court for final distribution.[1]

By later deeds, wills, orders, locations, and accomplishments, together with their abilities to maneuver through the English legal system, we can surmise who these people became.

With Abraham Piersey, cape merchant Anthony, John, William, Anthony, one woman.

At Captain William Pierce's residence Angelo.

At Kingsmills Plantation in Ye Neck of Woods Edward.

At Commander William Tucker's residence Antoney, Isabel (Isabella).

At Edward Bennett's plantation Anthony, Margaret, Frances, and Peter.

At Captain Francis West's plantation John Pedro, age thirty, who arrived in Virginia in 1623 on the *Swan* from England. John Pedro was one of three put on the *James* in Bermuda by Governor Butler and sent to England at the request of the Earl of Warwick.[2]

At Captain Matthews's plantation Jiro. Sometime after April 23, 1623, but before January 1624, Jiro died on the south side of the James River within the corporation of James City.[3]

George Yeardley, governor Three unnamed men and three unnamed women at Flowerdew, and two unnamed Africans at his residence in Jamestown.

List of the Living, February 16, 1623, Virginia[4]				
	Africans			
Master	Male	Female	Child	Total
G. Yeardley	3	5	0	8
A. Piersey	4	1	0	5
W. Tucker	1	1	0	2
W. Pierce	0	1	0	1
E. Bennett	1	2	1	4
S. Matthews	1	0	0	1
R. Kingsmill	1	0	0	1
Unknown (deceased)	0	0	0	1
Muster of Inhabitants, 1624–1625[5]				
	Africans			
Master	Male	Female	Child	Total
G. Yeardley	3	5	0	8
A. Piersey	4	2	1	7
W. Tucker	1	1	1	3
W. Pierce	0	1	0	1
E. Bennett	1	1	0	2
F. West	1	0	0	1
R. Kingsmill	1	0	0	1

Both recordings have a total of twenty-three Africans. However, there are several changes. Between 1623 and 1624–1625 we notice:

- Jiro, at Samuel Matthew's plantation has died. (–1)
- William Tucker, the child of Antoney and Isabel, has been born. (+1)

- Maria/Mary arrives from England and is listed at Bennett's plantation. (+1)
- Frances and Peter return to Abraham Piersey. (no change)
- Margaret disappears from the recording all together. (−1)

As mentioned, these early Africans rarely changed locations. In 1624–1625 Frances and Peter, who were recorded at Bennett's plantation, returned to Abraham Piersey's and were listed as a Negro woman with a young child of hers. The contracted exchange was Piersey's contribution for the lookout fort ordered to be built in 1622–1623 adjacent to Bennett's plantation. This location was the easternmost-settled point on the south side of the James River at Burwell Bay, a high point with a clear vantage overlooking the Chesapeake Bay to the north and east.[6] Another instance of location change was documented in the court case *Brasse v. Bass*. Brasse, protesting his master, was removed from Basse's Choice and placed with the governor's wife.[7] The court ordered his new master, the governor's wife, to pay him monthly for his services. In both instances, the movement was in direct response to contractual requirements.

The following Africans we can identify without question.

Antoney and Isabel Tucker

Antoney and Isabel (Isabella) were listed in the incorporation of Kecoughtan in William Tucker's household in February 1623 and in the Muster of 1624–1625. Antoney and Isabel eventually took the last name of Tucker from their master, Captain William Tucker, the commander of Point Comfort in 1619. The Tuckers have the distinction of becoming the first African family in the young English settlement of Virginia. Their son *William* was born by 1624 and became the first documented African child to be baptized in Virginia. Records show that William was the second documented African child in the early settlement.[8] William Tucker's descendants are among those buried at the Tucker Family Cemetery in today's Hampton, Virginia, where many of their descendants remain.

Frances

Frances, who became *Frances Driggers*, was the mother of the first documented African child in Virginia. Frances was listed as early as 1621 at Abraham Piersey's plantation, documented as a Negro woman with a young child of hers. We now know the young child to be Peter.[9] From the time of Piersey's death in 1627–1628[10] until 1633, Frances and the other Africans in Piersey's possession were moved to and from, caught up in the legal battle between Abraham Piersey's daughters and their stepmother, Frances Greville-West-Piersey, and then Matthews. Their stepmother had quickly married Captain Samuel Matthews after their father's death. As the administrator of Piersey's estate, the new Mrs. Frances Matthews removed the Africans from Floridew to Matthews' Manor.[11] In 1633 Elizabeth Piersey and her sister Mary Hill finally received their portion of their father's estate, and the Africans were returned to Piersey's daughters.

Sometime between 1635 and 1638, during the ouster of Governor John Harvey—Elizabeth Piersey's newlywed husband—the Africans were once again removed to Matthews' Manor. Matthews had led the charge to remove Governor Harvey and send him to England to stand in front of the king. During this time, the Flowerdew Africans were confiscated and distributed among Harvey's opponents. Frances was among those Africans.

At this point, Frances became the servant of Captain Francis Pott. Pott was a known participant in Governor Harvey's removal. Between 1638 and 1640 Frances married Emmanuel Driggers. Within the next fifteen years, as slavery manifested in Virginia, these two became some of the earliest freedom fighters in what eventually became the United States of America.[12] In addition to Peter, Frances had at least five biological and two adopted children with Emmanuel Driggers (see below).

By 1656 Frances had died in Northampton County, Virginia.[13]

Peter

Peter, who became known as *Peter George*, was the first documented African child in Virginia. Peter and his mother, Frances's, relocation to Bennett's plantation was one of very few relocations of the Africans recorded in colonial Virginia.[14] By 1623 Peter was listed with his mother as "young child of hers" located at Abraham Piersey's plantation in 1621–1622[15] and 1624–1625.[16] However, in 1623 they were at Bennett's plantation.[17] By 1640 Peter was found in Northampton County working for Nathaniel Littleton, where he was identified as a "Negro Carpenter."[18] He married Joan Johnson, daughter of Anthony Johnson.[19] They had two children, Jane and Anthony. In 1656 Peter's son, Anthony (Little Tony), and daughter, Jane, were listed in a will of Littleton's wife, Ann.[20] In 1664 Peter was again found taxable in the Littleton family, tithable under Francis Littleton in Northampton County.[21] Sometime during 1664–1665 Peter George, a carpenter, began working for Captain Francis Pigot (Piggot).[22] About 1676 Peter George received release from his indenture with the promise to pay ten thousand pounds of tobacco to his master. He completed the last payment in 1682.[23]

In 1684 Captain Francis Pigot, Littleton's kin, made his will in Northampton County, Virginia, listing Peter's son Anthony George.[24]

Margaret

Margaret, who became known as *Margaret Cornish*, was first documented at Bennett's plantation in the 1623 List of the Living and Dead. Bennett's plantation was settled just prior to the Native uprising of 1622. Following the devastating skirmish, Bennett's plantation was abandoned for at least six months.[25] How Margaret found herself on the south side of the James River at Bennett's plantation to begin with has been somewhat of a mystery. One possibility is that Margaret was one of two Africans seen castaway in the "depths of Somerset" with the crew of the *White Lion*.[26] When counting the numbers of their arrival in 1619–1620, two Africans do appear to have remained with Captain Jope on the *White Lion*.[27] Therefore, the circumstances and timing of Margaret's arrival at Bennett's plantation are murky. Perhaps she returned in May 1622 when the *White Lion* returned to Virginia and delivered "40 men and 40 head of cattle."[28]

Margaret's disappearance from Bennett's plantation was equally mysterious. In the 1624–1625 Muster, she simply vanishes. Perhaps her master was Robert Bennett and upon Bennett's death in late 1623 she went to live with Robert Chew and his family. In 1623 an unnamed African woman was living at John Chew's residence.[29] John Chew was the administrator of Robert Bennett's estate, which lends support and credibility to this conclusion.[30]

By 1636 Margaret was listed as a headright for Lieutenant Colonel Richard Cocke when he patented three thousand acres on the main river, in Charles City County. Sometime between 1638 and 1639 Margaret moved to Lieutenant Robert Sheppard's Chippokes Creek plantation on the south side of the James River with one child, a son named Mihill Gowen. Mihill's father, John Gowen (Gruyere), was living at a neighboring plantation patented by Captain William Ewens in 1619 known as the College Land.

In 1640, Margaret was found guilty of fornication with Robert Sweat, an English servant for Lieutenant Sheppard.[31]

October 17, 1640—Whereas Robert Sweat hath begotten with child a negro woman servant belonging unto Lieutenant

Sheppard, the court hath therefore ordered that the said negro woman shall be whipt at the whipping post and the said Sweat shall tomorrow in the forenoon do public penance for his offence at James City church in the time of divine service according to the laws of England in that case provided.[32]

Robert Sweat arrived on Robert Sheppard's plantation in 1638 from the *Guiding Star*.[33] After John Gowen severed their marriage in March 1641,[34] Margaret became the mother of at least four of Robert Sweat's children:

- Robert Cornish-Sweat, b. 1640[35]
- William Sweat, b. 1642, d. after 1711[36]
- Jane Sweat, b. April 1644; adopted by Emmanuel and Frances Driggers by April 1645[37]
- Anthony Cornish, b. 1645[38]

In February 1666 Margaret witnessed an indenture for Dorothy Thorne, who was to serve Charles Barham and his wife for a period of six years. This status certainly indicates that Margaret was not enslaved, because a slave could not witness a legal document. This also lends support to the conclusion that Margaret was a caretaker of some type—midwife, housekeeper, herbalist, or cook, but certainly not working in the field. In 1668, 1669, and 1670 Margaret was paying her own tithes in Lawnes Creek Parish on Hogg Island.[39] In October 1670 Margaret petitioned the General Court of Virginia to release her from paying taxes the following year, and the court granted her request due to poverty and her advanced age.[40]

John Gowen (Gruyere/Gaween)
John Gowen was one of the Africans taken from the *San Juan Bautista* and put aboard the *White Lion*. However, when the *White*

73

Lion arrived in August 1619, it's possible John did not disembark. John was perhaps one of the two Africans in Bermuda with the *White Lion* crew.[41] The other possibility is that he was taken to Bermuda aboard the *Treasurer* in September 1619 and was one of the few Africans sent to Warwick in England aboard the *James* in 1621. There is record of John, a Negro, arriving on the *James* from England in 1622 and his passage credited to William Ewens.[42] In either instance, John Gowen was one of the sixty Africans taken during the piracy of the *San Juan Bautista*.

By 1635 John had one child, a son named Mihill (Michael), with Margaret, who lived at an adjacent plantation. Then in March 1641 John opposed Margaret in the general court for custody of his son. John paid Margaret's master for Mihill's outstanding expenditure, and the court granted his request.[43] Within days, John indentured his son, Mihill, to Robert Stafford.[44] This one act not only assured Mihill's freedom but the freedom of his descendants for generations to come. By 1650 John had left Ewens's College Land, remarried, and had another child. Like Mihill, John's second son, Philip Gowen, born in 1650, traveled the same path of indenture to guarantee his freedom.[45]

During the course of his life, John Gowen confronted and won the fight for freedom. His fight didn't end with his own family. Records produce clear connections to many of the early Africans who found their paths to freedom. John was one of a handful of Africans who learned to maneuver the English legal system, using the courts to document the contractual agreements of their descendants and their possessions. Gowen's knowledge of the legal system also allowed him to become a magistrate, auditing and ruling over smaller filings. In York County, in his later years, John judged Europeans and Africans alike until his death. Upon his death, a new law was enacted that disavowed the ability of any African to adjudge any English man or woman.

John Gowen's children and grandchildren were as follows:[46]

- Mihill (Michael) Gowen, b. 1635[47]
  - William, b. August 25, 1655[48]
  - Daniel, b. ca. 1657[49]
  - Christopher, b. ca. 1658[50]
  - Thomas, b. ca. 1660[51]
- Philip Gowen, b. 1650[52]

Michael

Michael, who became *Michael Blizzard*, was probably on the *Treasurer* when she returned in March 1620. He is not found in any of the early musters or censuses. He was only listed in Captain William Ewens's patents.[53] Ewens was one of the largest landowners in early Virginia. His patents were continually renewed, ever since the original grant date of September 1619. Michael married Katherine (see below), and they became known as the Blizzards by the 1660s. It's been said they took their name after surviving the worst blizzard in Virginia's early history.

Katherine

Katherine was the wife of Michael Blizzard. Together they had at least five children living at the William Ewens plantation called the College Land on the south side of the James River. From a Surry County patent in 1659 that William Ewens's widow, Mary, renewed, she had fourteen hundred acres, including his land on the sunken marsh where the Blizzards lived. Listed in the patent are Michael and Katherine, together with the following children:

- Rebecca, b. ca. 1639
- Frances, b. ca. 1649

- Amos, b. ca. 1651
- Susanna, b. ca. 1654
- An unnamed child[54]

Descendants of Michael and Katherine Blizzard remain in Surry County, Virginia, to this day.

Mathew

Mathew was one of four Africans living in 1643 at Captain William Ewens's plantation known as the College Land.[55] Mathew may have been the unnamed African who was delivered to Ewens's plantation on the *Saker* in 1627. No further records have been discovered to date, and little else is known about Mathew.

Anthony (Toney King)

Anthony, who became *Toney King*, was one of four African men listed at Flowerdew Plantation between 1621 and 1628, at the time of Abraham Piersey's last will and testament. Caught in a legal battle between Piersey's widow and children, Toney King was moved to Denbigh Plantation on the north side of the James River when Piersey's widow married Samuel Matthews. Toney was noted in the 1660s as paying his own tithes and living in Northampton County, Virginia. Toney King had at least one daughter:[56]

- Sarah (dates unknown) married Richard Johnson, son of Anthony and Mary Johnson, Northampton County, Virginia.

William

William was one of four African men listed at Flowerdew Plantation between 1621 and 1628, until the time of Abraham Piersey's last will and testament.[57] Further information on William has not been found.

Anthony (Tony Longo)

Anthony, who became *Tony Longo*, was one of four African men sold to Abraham Piersey, the cape merchant, in 1619. He was documented at Piersey's plantation as early as 1621 and in 1623, 1624–1625, and until 1628, at which time Abraham Piersey's last will and testament was recorded.[58] In 1635 Tony Longo was one of the earliest Africans to be documented as "free," exactly seven years after the death of Piersey, his former master.

Tony Longo was ordered in 1647 to pay his debt of 384 pounds of tobacco to Francis White. If Longo would have been a slave, he wouldn't have been responsible for the debt; his master would have been. Longo had at least three children:

- Grace, b. ca. 1647
- Daughter, name unknown, b. ca. 1649
- James, b. ca. 1652

Longo and his wife, Catalina, purchased a 250-acre farm in March 1655.[59] Sometime after 1655, Longo's wife must have died, as she disappears from the records. From one notable case, the court portrayed Longo as a troublemaker, declaring that he led a lazy and evil life. In concern for his children, the court assigned Longo's children out "to preserve his offspring from his baleful influence." Undoubtedly, Longo had several misfortunes and possessed a harsh tongue, but whether he was a negligible father must have been in question. The court was apparently quite aware of Longo's freedom, making considerable requirements of his children's assignees. The "bigger girl" became an apprentice to a Captain George. The "youngest girl" went to Captain Edmund Bowman, and the boy, to Colonel Edmund Scarborough. The court gave special conditions to the children's appointed masters, requiring the girls "to be schooled in housewifery, spinning, knitting and such like and the boy to be put to shoemaking." Regardless, the order wouldn't go without a fight from Longo, and he eventually had a portion of the ruling overturned. Longo retained his eldest daughter, but the two younger children's placement was upheld. In 1660 Longo was responsible for only one tithe.[60] Longo's oldest daughter was named Grace, living with John Francisco in Northampton County, Virginia, in the 1660s.[61] Francisco worked with Longo in the early days at Flowerdew Plantation.

Records on Longo are found in Northampton County as well as Accomack County. In 1663 Northampton realigned its boundaries and split the northern third of the island. The northern portion became Accomack County. Longo lived on Pungoteague Creek on the northwestern shore.

John

John was one of four African men listed at Flowerdew Plantation between 1621 and 1628, at the time Abraham Piersey's last will and testament was recorded. He was one of several taken to the Matthews plantation when Governor Harvey was abducted to England. John became *John Francisco* of Northampton County, who married an African woman named Christian. John and Christian may have had no children of their own.

Juan/John Pedro

John Pedro, also called *Juan Pedro*, was one of three Africans taken from Bermuda to England in 1621; he was put aboard the *James* by Governor Nathaniel Butler and delivered to Leez Priory, the Earl of Warwick's estate in Felsted. John Pedro remained in England until early 1623, when a legal case drew increased attention to the *Treasurer*'s escapades with the Africans. John Pedro was put aboard the *Swan*, one of Warwick's ships, and smuggled out of England with Warwick's ally Francis West. John Pedro resurfaced at the New England Company's settlement, just north of Virginia, where the Earl of Warwick was heavily involved in the New England charter. From Plymouth he would go on to Weymouth with Captain Francis West and finally arrived in Virginia on the *Swan* in 1623. In the muster of 1624–1625 John Pedro was listed as a servant in the household of Captain Francis West.

John Pedro was a devout Catholic who never relinquished his religious teachings from his homeland.

Jiro

Jiro was listed in the List of the Living and Dead in 1623 at Captain Samuel Matthews's plantation on the south side of the James River at Hogg Island. By 1624 Jiro was dead.

Angelo/Angela/Angola

Angelo/Angela/Angola was one of three of the earliest Africans to reside at Jamestown, but it probably wasn't until 1622–1623, after the Native uprising on March 22, 1622. William Pierce, her master, patented 650 acres on Mulberry Island, where he resided from December 1619 until 1622, when he returned to Jamestown. Further, from 1623 to 1625 Angela was documented as living at William Pierce's residence at Jamestown. There are no records of Angela ever leaving Pierce's, marrying, or having children.

Edward

Edward was found at Kingsmill Plantation at Ye Neck of the Land, one mile north of Jamestown Island. Edward became *Edward Mozingo* and by 1641 had a son named Edward Mozingo Jr. in York County, Virginia.

Antonio and Maria

Antonio and *Maria* become known as *Anthony* and *Mary Johnson*. They both arrived in Virginia from England, courtesy of the Earl of Warwick. The likelihood that their passage was on the *San*

Juan Bautista remains strong, yet documentation to confirm this is sparse. They would have been aboard the *Treasurer* when she arrived in Bermuda in 1619 after mysteriously leaving Virginia. In 1621 Antonio and Maria were both put aboard Warwick's ship, the *James*, by Governor Nathaniel Butler in Bermuda and sailed for England.[62] When they reached the port of Southampton, they were taken directly to Warwick's estate of Leez Priory. Defiant to the Earl of Warwick's requests, Anthony quickly found himself back on the *James* and on his way to Virginia. By November 1621 Antonio's name had been anglicized to Anthony and he was at Edward Bennett's plantation on the south side of the James River overlooking Burwell Bay, the outermost post from England accessible to Warwick. Bennett was a devout Puritan and known loyal associate of the Earl of Warwick.

In March 1622 Anthony was one of a handful of settlers to survive the Native uprising responsible for slaughtering one-third of Virginia's overall population and killing more than fifty settlers at Bennett's plantation. For a time, the plantation would be abandoned. Within six months, after an agreement for a lookout fort to be built there, Bennett's plantation was reestablished.

Maria arrived in Virginia on the *Margaret and John* in late 1622 from England. Like Anthony, Maria anglicized her name to Mary, possibly camouflaging her Catholic heritage. By 1624 Mary was documented alongside Anthony on the south side of the James River at Bennett's Welcome in Warrasquarake. By 1635 Anthony and Mary were married and living at John Upton's plantation on the south side of the James, where they were listed as headrights. Upton had confirmed his patent with thirty-three headrights, which included two Africans: Anthony and Mary. Shortly thereafter, the Johnsons are documented as residents of the Eastern Shore.

On January 10, 1647, Anthony Johnson purchased a calf from James Berry,[63] by a deed proven in Northampton County,

Virginia. This purchase started the Johnsons' livestock venture, which quickly grew into a major monopoly on the Eastern Shore in Northampton County. In 1651 the Johnsons patented 250 acres at Great Naswattock Creek for the transportation of five persons, including their son Richard. The following year, the Johnsons' home was consumed by fire, and Mary and their two daughters were excused from paying taxes or tithes. The order read, "They have been Inhabitants in Virginia above thirty years . . . ordered that from the day of the date hereof (during their natural lives) the said Mary Johnson & two daughters of Anthony Johnson, Negro be disengaged and freed from payment of taxes."[64]

After rebuilding their home, Anthony and Mary continued to pay their own tithes and taxes and raised four children on the Eastern Shore:

- John, b. ca. 1631[65]
- Richard, b. ca. 1632[66]
- Joan, b. unknown, possible wife of Peter George[67]
- Daughter, b. unknown[68]

In 1653 Anthony Johnson took his servant, Casor, to court to fight his neighbor from confiscating him from Johnson's possession. Anthony won his case, but unfortunately for Casor, this court battle left him a servant to the Johnsons for all of his natural life.[69] By 1665 Anthony and Mary Johnson had sold their land in Northampton County, with the exception of fifty acres they left to their son Richard. Joining them in their move to Somerset County, Maryland, was their son John and his wife, Susanna, along with John Casor and fourteen head of cattle, a mare, and eighteen sheep.[70] It must be noted that the Johnsons moved to Maryland in the vicinity of Richard Bennett, Johnson's original master's kin, who exerted a heavy Puritan influence. In Maryland, many years later, Anthony and Mary's grandson owned a small plantation that he called Angola—a clear gesture to their heritage.

The Six Unnamed Africans at Governor Yeardley's
Possibilities are few. The three men and three women who were in Governor Yeardley's possession were never named. From association and an accumulation of other details, we can acknowledge those who were perhaps the men at Yeardley's, those who were perhaps the men at Yeardley's, but definitely of the *San Juan Bautista.*

Benjamin Doll
Benjamin Doll was among the first free Africans who lived on the south side of the James River in Lawnes Parish, Surry County, Virginia. In 1656, for the importation of six persons, Doll was granted a patent for 300 acres located on the south side of the Reeded Marsh lying east of the Blackwater River adjoining Captain Jordan's line.[71]

Doll, a respected African, was authorized and granted permission to act as attorney for Judah Hide in 1659. The following year he was a witness in a Surry County land deed.[72] Doll was probably the father of at least one son, John Doll (Daule), born about 1648.

John and his wife, Isabell, were Negro servants of Arthur Jordan until March 10, 1669, when they paid him to release them from any further service.[73] John Doll purchased 162 acres in Newport Parish, Isle of Wight County, from John Sojourner sometime after April 21, 1689.[74]

Paul Carter
Paul Carter was indentured to Nathaniel Littleton of Northampton County, Virginia, sometime prior to 1640.[75] Paul must have died by 1665, when his wife, Hannah, was released from her indenture prior to May of that year. Francis Payne and Emmanuel Driggus

promised Francis Pigot that they would support Paul's widow, if necessary.[76] For the years of 1668, 1671, 1675, and 1677, Carter's widow, Hannah, lived with Bashaw Farnando and his wife.[77] The following may have been the children of Paul and Hannah Carter:

- Edward,[78] b. ca. 1640
- Mary, b. ca. 1641
- James, b. ca. 1643
- Thomas, b. ca. 1645;[79] Thomas had the following children:[80]
  - Elizabeth, b. ?
  - Thomas, b. ?
  - Margaret, b. ?

Francis Payne/Pane

Francis was called "Francisco, a Negroe" when he was claimed as a headright in 1637 by Philip Taylor.[81] As early as 1649 he was listed as "Francis Payne, my Negro servant" when his master's widow, Jane Taylor-Eltonhead, recorded an order in the Northampton County Court stating that she gave him the rights to a crop he was raising and "power from tyme to tyme to make use of the ground and plantation" in return for fifteen hundred pounds of tobacco and six barrels of corn after harvest.[82] In July 1656 Jane Eltonhead confirmed Payne's freedom, stating,

> I Mrs. Jane Eltonhead . . . have hereunto sett my hand that ye aforesaid Payne shall be discharged from all hinderances of servitude or any that doth belong to ye sd Payne.[83]

Emmanuel Driggers

Emmanuel Driggers was possibly one of the six Africans found in Governor Yeardley's possession. Nevertheless Driggers was among the earliest Africans and should be known as one of

America's earliest freedom fighters. He possessed the knowledge to secure freedom for many Africans through the English legal system. Emmanuel married Frances, who was clearly documented as early as 1623 in Warrasquarake at Bennett's Welcome.[84] Sometime between 1628 and 1644, Emmanuel was indentured to Captain Francis Pott, commander of Point Comfort and owner of a large plantation on the Eastern Shore in Northampton County. In 1649 Emmanuel Driggers and his wife, Frances, were assigned by Pott to Stephen Charlton, to pay for Pott's debt to Charlton.

Emmanuel and Frances Driggers had at least seven children, two adopted and five biological:

- Elizabeth, b. ca. 1638 (adopted)[85]
- Frances, b. ca. 1640[86]
- Thomas, b. 1644[87]
- Jane, b. April 1644 (adopted)[88]
- Ann, b. 1648[89]
- Edward, b. 1650[90]
- William, b. 1655[91]

Emmanuel's wife, Frances, died before 1656, when he took a second wife named Elizabeth, an Englishwoman. With Elizabeth Driggers, Emmanuel had two more children:

- Devorax/Deverick, b. 1656[92]
- Mary, b. 1658[93]

Philip Mongom/Mongon

The name Mongom/Mongon was probably derived from the Bantu-speaking region of Mongo and was more than likely in recognition of Philip's heritage. Mongom was documented as a free man on January 30, 1648, by his master, William Hawley.[94] Like Anthony Johnson, Emmanuel Driggers, and Francis Payne, his fellow Angolans, Mongom raised some of the most sought-after livestock in Virginia. On June 27, 1678, he filed a notice trying to retrieve one of his prized horses, declaring the following:

> Notice is hereby given that I Philip Mungon have a light bay mare with a starr in the forehead, aged about 3 years, branded with a shipps hand, gone stray about seven months. If any person can give intelligence of the said mare, they shall be satisfyed for their care & expenses.[95]

Bashaw Farnando

In the late 1640s and 1650s Farnando was a servant for Captain Francis Pott on the Eastern Shore. Farnando was one of two Africans for whom Francis Pott testified, stating, "Emanuel Driggs and Bashaer Farnando, negroes, now servants, have certain cattle, hoggs and poultry, now in their possession." Farnando's holdings were quite impressive and would increase under his next master, Stephen Charlton. In December 1652 both Charlton and Pott swore under oath "these animals with their increase belonged to their negro servants":

> Whereas Capt. Francis Pott, Deceased, declared in his life time that when he departed this natural life . . . set his negro Bashaw Free but did not mention ye same in his will, know ye that I do by these presents sett ye said Bashaw att Liberty, proclaim him to be free from my servitude.[96]

The following are Africans who made great strides against the impending slave laws to remain free and must be noted.

Emmanuel Cumbo (Cambow)

Emmanuel Cumbo was listed in the early records, adjudged in September 1644 as a Christian servant and released from his contract in September 1665.[97] Emmanuel Cambow, "negro," was granted a patent of fifty acres in James City County on April 18, 1667.[98] His property ownership was a clue as to who Cumbo was. Very few and seemingly only those of the first-generation 1619 Africans and their descendants managed to maneuver through the English legal system to own property during Virginia's early years. Emmanuel Cumbo may have been the child named Manuel of an unnamed first-generation African woman and Hugh Davis, who was punished in 1630 for fornication with a member of the African community, and who was also made to apologize to the Africans after his whipping.[99]

John Phillip

John Phillip was not aboard the *San Juan Bautista* but made his way from England to Virginia in 1622 on the *James*. In 1624, after the court hearing of his baptism in England some twelve years earlier, John Phillip testified that he had sailed with known English privateer Captain Henry Mainwaring, who had seized a Spanish vessel years earlier.[100]

Brasse

Brasse was also not one of the *San Juan Bautista* Africans, yet he was in Virginia in 1625 and deserves mention for his early legal battle with his master. Brasse was brought to Virginia by a Captain Jones. After Jones's death, Brasse was contracted to Nathaniel Bass of Bass's plantation on the south side of the James River prior to 1625. Brasse took Nathaniel Bass to court for neglect and lack of substance. His contract required food, shelter, and clothes in exchange for his services, which was being denied in some respect. The court ordered Brasse to the custody of the governor's wife, who was required to pay Brasse a monthly wage for his employment.[101]

Notes

1. Piersey's last will and testament, Colonial Papers.

2. Governor Butler to the Earl of Warwick, October 9, 1620, in Ives, *Rich Papers*, 185–88*; Swan* manifest, available at https://www.packrat-pro.com/ships/shiplist.htm; Neill and Butler, "Virginia Carolorum."

3. McCartney, *Virginia Immigrants and Adventurers*, 423.

4. List of the Living and Dead, February 23, 1623.

5. Hecht, "Virginia Muster," 78.

6. Author's observation.

7. *Brasse v. Nathaniel Bass of Basse's Choyce*, Minutes of the General Council, 1625.

8. 1625 Muster, William Tucker's residence.

9. Sarah Driggers made a deposition in the case of Peter George during the May 29, 1691, session of the Northampton County Court (Orders 1689-98, 116). Sarah King, who was married to Thomas Driggers (b. 1644), son of Emmanuel and Frances Driggers, named Peter George as her brother (i.e., brother to her deceased husband, Thomas Driggers).

In the 1623 List of the Living and Dead, a Negro woman with a young child of hers was transferred to Bennett's plantation after the uprising as Piersey's contribution to the lookout fort. In the 1624–1625 Census, Frances and Peter have disappeared, and the Negro woman with the young child of hers has reappeared.

10. Piersey's last will and testament, Colonial Papers.

11. Mary Hill, executor of the Abraham Piersey estate, sued Captain Samuel Matthews for her father's remaining estate after the death of Frances Greville-West-Piersey-Matthews in 1633.

12. Pott's agreement recorded in Northampton County shows Emmanuel Driggers's adoptive daughter Jane indentured to him until she reached the age of thirty. In 1652 the release of Jane Driggers was recorded as paid in full by her adoptive father, Emmanuel Driggers.

13. According to a Northampton County recording, Emmanuel Driggers had remarried an Englishwoman by the name of Elizabeth in 1656 (Northampton County Records).

14. See page 56, note 35, this volume.

15. Piersey's Tolle 1621.

16. The 1624–1625 Census of Virginia shows them located at Piersey's recently purchased Floridew Plantation, previously owned by Governor Yeardley.

17. List of the Living and Dead, February 23, 1623.

18. Turman and Lewis, "Will of Ann Littleton."

19. Bell, *Northampton County Virginia Tithables*, 59, shows Peter George along with his wife, Joan/Joane, tithable under Captain Pigot.

20. Turman and Lewis, "Will of Ann Littleton."

21. Northampton County Records (Deeds and Wills, 1657–66, 174–75).

22. Bell, *Northampton County Virginia Tithables*, 13–15.

23. Northampton County Records, Deeds, Wills, Orders 1680–92, 53; Deal, *Race and Class*, 444.

24. Northampton County Records, Deeds, Wills, Orders 1680–92, 53; Deal, *Race and Class*, 444.

25. Boddie, "Edward Bennett"; Edward Bennett's letter to the Virginia Council dated October 1622 requested that the tenants of Bennett's plantation be allowed to return.

26. Manchester Papers, 252.

27. Kingsbury, *Records*, 3:639.

28. Ibid.

29. Nugent, *Cavaliers and Pioneers*.

30. "Minutes . . . 1622–1629 (Continued)."

31. Robinson, "Virginia Council and General Court Records."

32. Ibid. A general law against fornication applied to all members of the colony. In other cases, the woman, regardless of race, was whipped, with the man receiving a lesser punishment. Also note that she is called a servant—not a slave (see also McIlwaine, *Minutes of the Council*).

33. Coldham, *English Adventurers and Emigrants* (1638 patent for 650 acres on the Chippokes Creek, James City, Virginia); Nugent,

Cavaliers and Pioneers; Robinson, "Virginia Council and General Court Records," 281; Foley, *Early Virginia Families*, 21.

34. McIlwaine, *Minutes of the Council*, 477.

35. Ibid.

36. William Sweat was twenty-five years old in March 1667/68 when he made a deposition on behalf of his master, Thomas Binns (Surry County Court Records 2:305; 3:2). William was taxable in Francis Mason's Surry County household in Lower Chippokes, Lawnes Creek Parish, in 1674 and 1675 and taxable in Thomas Binns's household from 1680 to 1684. William paid his own taxes from 1685 to 1703. In December 1711 William was exempted from payments of public tax because of old age (Surry County Court Records, 3:250, 278). (His birth year reflects calendar changes in Great Britain at the time.)

37. On May 27, 1645, Emmanuel Driggers bound his adoptive daughter Jane to Captain Francis Pott to serve him until the age of thirty-one. She was not Driggers's natural daughter, as her indenture states that Emmanuel Driggers "bought and paid for her to Robt Sheppard" (Northampton County Records, Deeds, Wills, 1645–51, 82).

38. In September 1696 Anthony Cornish was security for Margaret Sweat's administration on the estate of Robert Sweat (Surry County Court Records).

39. Surry County Court Records, 2:340, 314, 372.

40. McIlwaine, *Minutes of the Council*, 225; Heinegg, *Free African Americans*, 1:354–55.

41. Manchester Papers, 252.

42. Ferrar Papers, Reel 2, #400.

43. McIlwaine, *Minutes of the Council*; Robinson, "Virginia Council and General Court Records," notes.

44. "Release of Indenture of Mihill Gowen, Negro, of late serving my brother Xtopher Stafford, dcsd, by his last will & testament, had his freedom given him after the expiration of 4 years of service

to my uncle, Robert Stafford. I, Anne Barnhouse do absolve, quit and discharge the said Mihill Gowen from my service 25 October 1657. A. B. X" (the mark of Anne Barnhouse) (York County Records, 1657–1659, book 3, 16, 18).

45. Indenture in Warwick County (Colonial Papers, microfilm p. 19); Amye Beazleye's will; McIlwaine, *Minutes of the Council*, 411; 50 acres, Quit Rent Roll, James City County.

46. Heinegg, *Free African Americans*, 543–44.

47. Robinson, "Virginia Council and General Court Records."

48. Baptism, September 25, 1655, York County Records, 3:16.

49. Kingston Parish; Gloucester County Records, Patents 6:679, 9:147.

50. Abingdon Parish; Gloucester County Records, Register 319.

51. Westmoreland County Records, Orders 1693, 1702.

52. Colonial Papers, microfilm p. 19, folio 2.

53. Nugent, *Cavaliers and Pioneers*, 146.

54. "1659 Mrs Ewen held 1400 acres of land, 7 negroes, 50 head of cattle, 15 hogs, etc." (Boddie, *Colonial Surry*). Kingsbury, *Records*, vol. 4; LVA Microfilm Reel #113; Surry County Records (1652–1673), 154.

55. Nugent, *Cavaliers and Pioneers*.

56. Northampton County Records, Orders, Wills, Etc., 1674–1679, microfilm no. 27, p. 247.

57. List of the Living and Dead, February 23, 1623; 1625 Muster, Abraham Piersey's Flowerdew Plantation.

58. Colonial Papers.

59. Northampton County Records, Records, Deeds, Wills, 1654–1668.

60. Northampton County Records, Orders 1647–64, 102.

61. Bell, *Northampton County Virginia Tithables*; Breen and Innes, *"Myne Owne Ground,"* 68, 77, 80, 83–86, 94, 99–100, 105, 111.

62. Hashaw, *Birth of Black America*.

63. Northampton County Records, Deeds, Wills, Orders, 1651–1654, 123.

64. Northampton County Records, Deeds, Wills, Orders, 1651–1665, fol. 161.

65. John Johnson received a grant for 550 acres in Northampton County on May 10, 1652, adjacent to 250 acres granted to Anthony Johnson (Northampton County Records, Patents 3:101; Deeds and Wills, 1657–1666, 57–58, 103; Deeds and Wills, 1651–54, fol. 200).

66. Governor Richard Bennett instructed Nathaniel Littleton to deliver one black cow to Richard Johnson, February 8, 1653. In 1652 Richard claimed two headrights, and on November 21, 1654, he received a patent for 100 acres in Northampton County adjoining his father and his brother John's property (Northampton County Records, Deeds, Wills, Orders, 1651–1654, fol. 103, p. 133; Patents, 1652–1656, 290).

67. One of two daughters of Mary Johnson was excused from paying taxes after a fire destroyed the Johnson home in 1653. Joan received 100 acres adjacent to her brother John Johnson in Northampton County (Whitelaw, *Virginia's Eastern Shore*, 671). Edward Littleton mentioned Peter; his wife, Joan; and their daughters, Jane and Susan, in Littleton's will of 1663.

68. One of two unnamed daughters excused from paying taxes after a fire destroyed the Johnson home in 1653 (Northampton County Records).

69. Northampton County Records, Deeds, Wills, Orders, 1651–1665, 226.

70. Accomack County Records, Deeds and Wills, 1664–1671, fol. 10; p. 12, fol. 12.

71. Surry County Records, Patents Book 4:71–72.

72. Surry County Records, Deeds, Orders, 1:146, 156.

73. Ibid.

74. Isle of Wight County Records, Deed Book 7:217.

75. Northampton County Records, Orders 1640–1645, 42.

76. Northampton County Records, Deeds and Wills, 1665–1668, pt. 2, 15.

77. Bell, *Northampton County Virginia Tithables*.

78. Northampton County Records, Deeds, Wills, 1657–1666, 174–75.

79. Ibid.

80. Northampton County Records, Wills and Orders, book no. 13, 1689–1698; Colonial Papers, microfilm no. 27a, 250.

81. Nugent, *Cavaliers and Pioneers*, 1:74.

82. Northampton County Records, Deeds and Wills, 1651–1654.

83. Northampton County Records, Deeds and Wills, 1654–1655, 100.

84. Frances was listed in the List of the Living and Dead at Warrasquarake in February 1623 with her son Peter, Margaret, and Anthony, all Negroes. This association would remain strong among their descendants for generations.

85. Elizabeth was listed as one of two girls indentured to Frances Potts on May 27, 1645 (Northampton County Records, Deeds and Wills, 1645–1651, 82). This Elizabeth may be the Elizabeth Key who acquired her release in the 1660s.

86. Frances received a bay mare from her father, Emmanuel, in 1673. In 1678 Frances recorded her livestock mark in court (Northampton County Records, Deeds and Wills, 1651–1654, 16).

87. Thomas was one of Emmanuel and Frances's children who never found his freedom. From 1664 to 1667 he was taxable in Thomas Poynter's household. In 1666 he was judged guilty of fornication with Sarah King, whom he married within the year. Lieutenant Colonel William Kendall complained that Thomas was still a slave belonging to him and that he was neglecting his master when John Francisco and Francis Payne, Negroes, complained Thomas was abusing them. The court ordered twenty lashes, and shortly after, Thomas's child, who was then indentured to Kendall, became indentured to John Francisco until the age of twenty-one (Northampton

County Records, Orders 11664-74, fol. 30, fol. 52, 53). See also Heinegg, *Free African Americans*, 1:425–37.

88. On May 27, 1645, Emmanuel Driggers bound Jane to Captain Francis Pott to serve him until the age of thirty-one. She was not the natural daughter of Driggers, as her indenture states that Emmanuel Driggers "bought and paid for her to Robt Sheppard" (Northampton County Records, Deeds and Wills, 1645–1651, 82). The only known African associated with Captain Robert Sheppard in 1645 was Margaret Cornish. Therefore, we can conclude that Jane's parents were Margaret Cornish and Robert Sweat. Margaret certainly had a connection to Frances Driggers, wife of Emmanuel. See the afterword.

89. Ann was ten years old when she was sold to John Pannell. Pannell left her to his daughter Hannah Pennell by his will dated December 18, 1660 (Northampton County Records, Deeds and Wills, 1655–1668, 78).

90. Edward was sold to Henry Armitrading in 1657 at the age of three (Northampton County Records, Deeds and Wills, 1655–1668, 74). See also Heinegg, *Free African Americans*, 1:426–28.

91. On March 1679 the Northampton County Court ordered William to receive twenty lashes together with his wife, Alice, fifteen lashes for killing a hog belonging to their neighbor (Northampton County Records, Orders, 1678–1683, 3). By February 1693 William was deceased when Ralph Pigot reported to the Northampton County Court that William was indebted to him for 800 pounds of tobacco and Thomas Taylor was indebted to William for eight pairs of shoes (Northampton County Records, Orders and Wills, 1689–1698, 261). See also Heinegg, *Free African Americans*, 1:426.

92. Heinegg, *Free African Americans*, 1:426.

93. Ibid.

94. Northampton County Records, Deeds and Wills, 1654–1655, January 30, 1648, recorded October 29, 1654, Library of Virginia microfilm no. 4, p. 54. "Know all these men by these presents that I Wm Hawley . . . Philip Mongom be a free man."

95. Northampton County Records, Deeds, Orders, Wills, Etc., 1674–1679, June 27, 1678, Library of Virginia microfilm no. 27, p. 273.

96. William Kendall, May 30, 1659 (Northampton County Records, Deeds, Wills, 1657–1666, p. 57).

97. "Randolph Manuscript," 232.

98. Northampton County Records, Patents, 1667, 6:39.

99. Hening, *Statutes*, 1:146.

100. McIlwaine, *Minutes of the Council*, 33.

101. *Brasse v. Nathaniel Bass of Basse's Choice* (General Court Records, 1625).

11

Slavery vs. Servitude

The Virginia Company of London had held the charter on the Virginia settlement since 1607. The rules and laws were regulated by the leaders and investors of the Company yet conformed to England's rule. In 1619–1620 no laws in England, Virginia, or Bermuda used the word "slavery." When the *San Juan Bautista* Africans were brought to the shores of Point Comfort, they were traded to the governor and cape merchant. The trade wasn't much different than for those arriving from England and indenturing themselves to pay for their passage, except for two aspects: they were maritime contraband stolen from a Spanish slaver, and many of them were juveniles.

Within months of their arrival, a legal battle had ensued. Gondomar, the Spanish ambassador to the court of King James I of England, brought accusations against the Virginia Company of London of piracy and theft of sixty Africans belonging to his

95

family. Eventually the Earl of Warwick's ship the *Treasurer* was named, and witnesses from her crew were called to testify.[1] The two sides clashed, and the power struggle between two influential aristocrats had begun. Until this case was resolved or dismissed, the Africans would retain their ambiguous status of maritime contraband, which is indeed where it remained until Gondomar's death in 1626.

Even if their status as maritime contraband was discounted, the age factor was the next hurdle. Orphans, abandoned children, and underage arrivals from England found themselves bound out until a mandated legal age. For consideration of the issue of the Africans' age in these matters, the Somers Isles Company of Bermuda offers a true comparison. Bermuda was operating under the same type of English charter as Virginia, with many of the Company's members investing in both charters.

The earliest records show that the word "slave" was used without regard to race. In 1617, the Africans in Bermuda were noted as "tenants" working on Company land. Under the Bermuda Company, it seems slavery was seen as a punishment for all wrongdoers. For instance, "Symon, the Negro," was "condemned to be a slave to the Colony during the Governor's pleasure for assaulting a child."[2] At the same court, an Englishman was sentenced to be "a slave unto the colony" for aiding the governor's opposing faction. Laborers—whether English, African, or Native—were servants bound or hired to serve a certain master, but they were not enslaved. Therefore, during this period, even the meaning of the word "slave" was questionable, when in 1621 it was written "they were as free as any other servants" in Bermuda.[3]

At no other time were the Africans' skills more apparent to the needs of the settlement than in the rebuilding period of Virginia in 1622–1623 after the Native uprising of 1622. In the aftermath— with one-quarter of Virginia's population dead, the crops burned, and the livestock killed or confiscated—the remaining settlers from the eighty plantations up and down the James River were huddled together for a secure defense at eight of them. With the lack of skilled workers and servants with any type of experience, the Africans would have replanted the crops and managed the livestock, ensuring the availability of food during the rebuilding in the months and years ahead. The first generation of Africans were working in the service of the planters, living side by side among indentured servants. Together they ate, slept, and worked, as the Africans taught the European servants and the continual string of newcomers how to grow many crops. The knowledge of the Africans and the contributions they made in the years following allowed the withered English settlement of Virginia to survive and eventually thrive. In fact, the Africans must have held some sort of respectable status, because in 1630, Hugh Davis, an Englishman, was ordered to be whipped after apologizing to the entire African community for lying with one of their own.[4]

The Africans' knowledge became irreplaceable, much too valuable for the planters to lose when their eventual indentures were complete. For over a decade, the 1619 Africans had provided the knowledge and skills that enriched the most established and profitable of the planters.

As the years crept along and the colony expanded, by the end of the 1630s and early 1640s, and with the legalization of slavery to the north in the Massachusetts Colony, the laws regarding the African community in Virginia had begun to harden.[5] These laws made it tremendously difficult for Africans to leave the employ of their European masters.[6] With each and every legal battle where the Africans prevailed, new laws were quickly set in place by the European powers to eradicate any newfound avenue to freedom. During these times, the deadliest sins of evil prevailed, and slavery began to rear its ugly head.

The Africans needed to use the English court system to protect their children, land, and livestock, as well as their fruitful trades.

The following transaction records provide good examples regarding the Africans' ability to trade; regardless if it was between father and son, two Africans, or an African and an Englishman, they recorded transactions in such a manner as to guarantee payment and transfer:

> John Gossall, negro shall forthwith make payment unto Francis Payne, negro ye sum & quantity of one thousand four hundred pounds of tobacco.[7]
>
> . . .
>
> I Anthony Johnson negro doe assign and surrender all my right to ye cow marked, two heifers of a yeares old and two yearling heifers & one calfe to my son John Johnson negro.[8]
>
> . . .
>
> I John Johnson negro bargain and make sale of a black cow unto Edward Martin.[9]
>
> . . .
>
> Frances Payne of Northampton County, Negro have bargained sold & delivered unto Anthony Johnson a mare colt for and in consideration of 2,200 pounds of tobacco and caske. 31 January 1659. Francis (X—his mark) Payne. Witnesses: William Kendall, Edward Littleton.[10]

Anthony Johnson secured testimony from a white neighbor to clarify his son John's identity:

> These are to certify and declare that I Edmond Scarborough caused a patent of four hundred and fifty acres of land adjoining a tract of land of 250 acres granted to Anthony Johnson bounded on the south part at the maine creek. . . .

John Johnson negro whose name being the same as John Johnson joyner still pretends to a right . . . has no relation to John Johnson Negro whose patent it is.[11]

The case of William Harman, husband of the free woman Jane Driggers, was exceptional. Even with contracts being recorded, we find instances where they are challenged. In 1659 we note Harman being transferred to William Kendall from his master's widow.

In consideration of ye sum of 4,000 pounds of good tobacco & cask in hand paid, bargained and sold unto William Kendall one negro man called by ye name of William Harman which Negro came properly to be my owne goods & chattel by marriage with wife Mary, ye executrix and relict of Col. Wm Andrews deceased.[12]

In Northampton County, Virginia, Francis Payne, a Negro, living upon Colonel William Kendall's property, married an Englishwoman named Amy, who after Payne's death remarried an Englishman, William Gray. Between 1660 and 1671 William Harman remained indentured to Kendall and was living upon Kendall's land, lent to Francis Payne, a Negro freeman.

Harman must have been a kind soul, as he, and undoubtedly his wife, Jane, took care of a bastard child not his own for over a year. This case also shows that the legal requirement of bondage of any child wasn't less than twenty-five years.

On the 7th of December 1674, Nicholas Silvedo being convicted as ye reputed father of a bastard child, for the saving of the parish harmless from which care, was committed to ye custody of Mr. Jno Culpeper late High Sheriff of this County until he should enter into bond to perform the same, and he having escaped out of said High Sheriff's custody, and the said child since kept by Wm Harman negro thirteen months, it is ordered that Mr. Jno. Robins ye present high sheriff detayne 1200 pounds of tobacco and cask in his hands of the late sheriff's and make payment thereof unto ye said Wm Harmon for ye keeping of ye said child. And for as much as ye said Harman desired to be discharged from keeping ye said child any longer, ordered proclamation be made for any person to take ye said child till 24 years of age.[13]

Then, on July 29, 1675, the following complaint was filed:

Whereas Amy, the wife of Wm Gray hath complained to ye Court that her said husband hath made away almost all her estate and also hath in a gross manner beat her & abused her and she suspects that he intended to destroy what he can of that which is left & so to remove away and leave her upon the parish for relief . . . conveyed a mare from his plantation. . . . Sheriff take him into custody.[14]

One month later, the following eviction was filed:

Said difference between Col. Wm Kendall and Wm Gray who married Amy ye relict of Francis Paine Negro, deceased, to whom the said Coll. Kendall let a parcel of land & tenements under several conditions which not only she the said Amy but also the sd Wm Gray having failed to perform, therefore . . . were by consent of the Court evict the said Wm Gray and Amy his wife from the said land.[15]

By the end of 1675, William Harman was a free man. Listed in the Northampton County Tithables were William Harman and his wife, Jane (Sweat-Driggers-Gossall), paying their own tithes and free from indenture.[16]

As the laws to alienate the Africans progressed, in 1691 Virginia banned all interracial marriages, threatening to exile whites who married Africans and their descendants. This law was enacted because the earlier laws of status ran with the status of the mother. In the seventeenth century, exile would have functioned as a death sentence.

Whereas in 1684 Sarah Dawson servant to Mr. Jno Eyre being summoned to answer the presentation of the Grand Jury for fornication and having by her own confession acknowledged in open court that she had had three bastard malotto children by her said master's Negro slave Peter, she would serve six additional years & receive twenty-one lashes.[17]

. . .

On the petition of Sarah the white wife of Peter Beckett, slave to Mr. John Eyre, ordered that her child is at her own dipose, she finding sufficient security to save the parish harmless from the said child, and also she satisfy the said John Eyre for what shall be reasonably due her from his charge, expenses and trouble of his house about the said child from its birth to the time of her placing it out. July 1689.[18]

. . .

Sheriff summons Sarah Dawson servant to Mr. Jno. Eyre for fornication.[19]

. . .

Grand Jury presentments: Sarah Dawson for fornication.[20]

During the seventeenth century, free Africans on the Eastern Shore who shared and fulfilled the same aims and objectives as whites were no anomaly. In the 1668 Northampton County Tithables, over one-third of the people listed were free Negroes. If they did not escape the hand of slavery, they continued to live and work under very similar conditions as the white servants.

Notes

1. Preliminary questioning of the *Treasurer*'s captain, Privy Council; Hashaw, *Birth of Black America*.

2. Bernhard, "Beyond the Chesapeake."

3. Governor Butler to Sir Nathaniel Rich, January 12, 1621, in Ives, *Rich Papers*, 229.

4. Hening, *Statutes*, 1:146.

5. Virginia General Court Records; see a 1639 case of three runaway servants, including one African.

6. January 1640: all people "except negroes" are to be provided with firearms and ammunition; October 1629: "All those that worke in the ground of what quality or condition soever, shall pay tithes to the minister"; March 1643: "Changes in Tax/Tithables. All males, both European and Negro, of the age of 16 yrs and older and all Negro Females 16 years of age and older shall be taxable"; February 1645: All men between the ages of 16 and 60, and all African men and women shall be tithable; March 1658: Tax/Tithes Law changes. All male servants and all Negro males and females shall be considered tithable; December 1662: Condition of the Mother: General Assembly declared all children born in this country shall be held in bond or free only according to the mother's condition; September 1667: Legislation for slavery was further ensured when a law was enacted stating that the status of baptism no longer can alter the person's bondage or freedom. See Hening, *Statutes*.

7. Northampton County Records, Deeds, Wills, 1654–1655, LVA microfilm, no. 4, fol. 138.

8. Northampton County Records, Deeds, Wills, 1654–1655, August 31, 1659, recorded October 21, 1659, LVA microfilm, no. 4.

9. Northampton County Records, Deeds, Wills, 1654–1655, July 29, 1658, recorded October 21, 1659, LVA microfilm, no. 4.

10. Northampton County Records, Deeds, Wills, 1654–1655, LVA microfilm, no. 4, p. 74.

11. Northampton County Records, Deeds, Wills, 1654–1655, June 1653, recorded October 21, 1659, LVA microfilm, no. 42, pp. 57–58.

12. Northampton County Records, Deeds, Wills, 1654–1655, July 13, 1659, William Smart, recorded January 31, 1659/60, LVA microfilm, no. 4, p. 70.

13. Northampton County Records, Orders, Wills, Etc., 1674–1679, LVA microfilm, no. 27, p. 12.

14. Ibid., 59.

15. Ibid., 69–70.

16. Northampton County Records, List of Tithables for 1675, 74.

17. Northampton County Records, Wills, Orders, 1683–1689, LVA microfilm, no. 27, p. 59 (1684).

18. Ibid., 442, 443 (1689).

19. Ibid., 47.

20. Ibid., 27, p. 53.

1619

LUANDA, AFRICA TO VIRGINIA

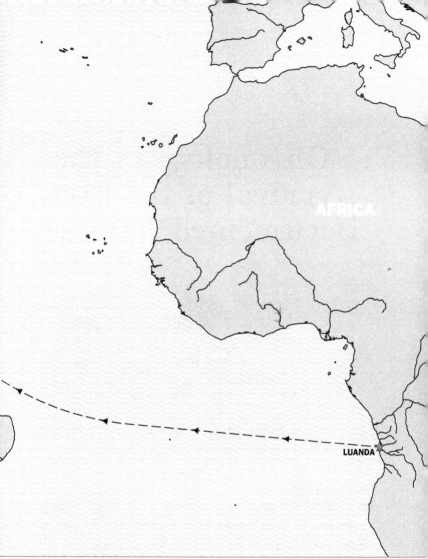

AFRICA

LUANDA

© First Freedom Publishing

KEY

— — — — — — — — — — SAN JUAN BAUTISTA

— ·· — ·· — ·· — ·· — TREASURER

— · — · — · — · — WHITE LION

Chronology of the Arrival of the First Documented Africans

The following chronology outlines the status of the first Africans in the earliest years of Colonial Virginia.

Summer 1619

The *San Juan Bautista*, a Spanish galleon sailing to the port of Veracruz with a full underbelly of enslaved Africans, is fired upon by two English corsairs in the Bay of Campeche. The two English corsairs take sixty Africans and sail for Virginia. Note: The *Bautista* was a Spanish galleon–type warship built in Japan in 1613. This type of warship was not known to transport slaves. Therefore, one would have to conclude the two English corsairs were searching for Spanish treasure, not slaves.

Mid-August 1619

The *White Lion* arrives in Somerset, at the southwestern tip of Bermuda. Four crewmen and two Africans are sent ashore to find relief. The party is quickly detained and their request for entry into the harbor denied. The *White Lion* disappears.

Late August 1619

The *White Lion* arrives on the shores of Point Comfort, where the English captain Jope, sailing under the Dutch/Flemish marque, exchanged "20, & odd" Africans to the governor and cape merchant for victuals.

The *Treasurer* arrives four days later. Due to an expired marque, Point Comfort's commander William Tucker sends for the governor's permission for the *Treasurer* to land and sell her cargo. As the governor's men William Ewens and William Pierce return to bring the English ship upriver to Jamestown, the *Treasurer* is sailing out into the Atlantic.

September 15, 1619

Captain William Ewens patents four hundred acres on the south side of the James River based on his recently landed headrights. Four Africans are eventually associated with this property.

October 1619

The *Garland* arrives in Bermuda from a long and sickening journey to Virginia, to replenish its supply and allow its passengers to recover.

October 20, 1619

The *Treasurer* arrives in Bermuda, bringing "29 Negros, 2 chestes of graine, 2 chests of wax, a smale quantity of tallow, little worth."

Due to the *Treasurer*'s expired commission from the Duke of Savoy, ownership of the Africans is an ambiguous legal matter to be settled at a later date.

November 1619
A hurricane hits Bermuda and destroys the *Warwick*, which had brought the newest governor to Bermuda a month prior. The *Warwick* had been contracted by the Company to send Bermuda's tobacco harvest to England.

In the governor's meeting with his council, Governor Butler orders the *Garland*'s captain to return to England with the Company's crop and the *Treasurer* to take the *Garland*'s passengers on to Virginia in her stead. Governor Butler then orders the *Treasurer* to be rigged and refit.

Bermuda's governor Butler removes the Africans from Warwick's land, where Kendall had placed them upon their arrival.

By February 1620
The *Treasurer* has left Bermuda on its return journey to Virginia, carrying approximately eighteen Africans.

March 1620
Census shows thirty-two Africans in the settlement of Virginia, fifteen men and seventeen women.

1621
In Bermuda, Governor Butler places at least three Africans—Antonio, Maria, and Juan Pedro—aboard the *James*, bound for England. Five weeks later, the *James* arrives at the port of Southampton, and the three are taken to the Earl of Warwick's great manor at Leez Priory in Felsted, Essex.

Late 1621

Antonio arrives in Virginia on the *James* from England and is placed on Bennett's plantation. Anthony/Antonio is questioned about the *San Juan Bautista* piracy by the Privy Council, but his testimony is dismissed as it contradicts Elfrith's. Anthony's testimony is removed under questioning about his baptism.

March 22, 1622

The Native uprising.

February 1623

The List of the Living and Dead shows the following Africans in the Virginia settlement:

Four at Warrasquarake: Anthony (Antonio, arrived on the *James*), Margaret, Peter, and Frances. Peter and Frances are one and the same as the "Negro woman with young child of hers" listed in Piersey's residence, before and after the building of the lookout fort adjacent to Bennett's Welcome on the south side of the James River. In the 1625 muster, Peter and Frances are no longer listed by name, and the Negro woman with young child of hers returns to Piersey.

Eleven living at Flowerdew (recently purchased by Piersey): Five of these Africans—Two Anthonys, John, William, and an unnamed Negro woman—are Piersey's, and the other six are Governor Yeardley's, contracted to Dr. Woodson. Dr. Woodson and his wife, Sarah, were living at Flowerdew.

Two unnamed persons living at George Yeardley's residence in Jamestown.

Two living at William Tucker's household: Antony and
Isabella.

One living at Ye Neck of Land in the Kingsmills residence:
Edward.

One living at the Matthews plantation near James City: Jiro.

One living at the treasurer's plantation: Angelo/Angela.

One listed as dead.

By February 1625

Baby William Tucker is born to Isabella and Antony in Tucker's
residence.

John Pedro arrives on the *Swan* in 1623 and is living on the
Eastern Shore.

Maria/Mary, who arrived from England on the *Margaret and
John* after the 1622 massacre, is eventually recorded at Bennett's
Welcome by 1624.

Peter and Frances at Bennett's Welcome return to Piersey's
Floridew Plantation as "Negro woman with young child of hers."

Angela/Angelo is in Jamestown at Captain William Pierce's
residence. Pierce and Angela/Angelo were living at the treasurer's
plantation in 1623.

September 1625

Lady Temperance Yeardley receives temporary custody of Brasse,
a Negro man sold to Captain Nathaniel Bass by Captain Jones.
Lady Yeardley is ordered to pay Brasse forty pounds of tobacco
per month while he is in her employ. On October 3, 1625, the
court gives Governor Francis Wyatt custody of Brasse.

1626

Gondomar, the Spanish ambassador to the court of King James I
of England, dies. Within the year, the legal remnants of the case
involving the Africans pirated in 1619 are dismissed.

1627

The ship *Saker* arrives in Virginia delivering nothing but one African to William Ewens's plantation on the south side of the James known as the College Land. (By 1627 William Ewens had patented one thousand acres of land.)

Abraham Piersey died and his seven Africans became the property of Piersey's widow, the recently remarried Frances Piersey-Matthews, who was to make sale of his servants.

1628

The last will and testament of Sir George Yeardley requires his eight Africans to be sold. They aren't listed as chattel, slaves, or servants but in a separate ambiguous class of their own: Negroes.

The *Fortune*, captained by Arthur Guy, arrives in Jamestown with one hundred Angolans stolen from a Spanish vessel.

October 1629

Changes to the laws take place regarding Africans: "All those that worke in the ground of what quality or condition soever, shall pay tithes to the minister."

1630

For laying with a Negro, Englishman Hugh Davis is whipped and made to apologize before an assembly of Negroes and others.

1635

Tony Longo is declared a free man by his employer when Nathaniel Littleton testifies to his freedom "by a certen wrytinge under my hand."

1635–1638

African men and woman begin to be used as headrights, suggesting servitude.

January 1640

Additional changes take place in the laws against Negroes. All people "except negroes" are to be provided with firearms and ammunition.

July 1640

Three runaway servants are retrieved from Maryland: a Dutchman, a Scot, and a Negro, John Punch/Bunch. The two Europeans receive additional time added to their contracts for their punishment. John Punch/Bunch receives additional service for the time of his natural life here or elsewhere.

October 17, 1640

"Whereas Robert Sweat hath begotten with child a negro woman servant belonging unto Lieutenant Sheppard, the court hath therefore ordered that the said negro woman shall be whipt at the whipping post and the said Sweat shall tomorrow in the forenoon do public penance for his offence at James City church in the time of divine service according to the laws of England in that case provided." (There was a general law against fornication that applied to all members of the colony. In other cases, the woman, regardless of race, was whipped, with the man receiving a lesser punishment. Also, this woman was a servant—not a slave.

March 31, 1641

Suit of John Gowen: "Whereas it appeareth to the court that John Gowen, being a negro servant unto William Ewens, was permitted by his said master to keep hogs and make the best benefit thereof to himself provided that the said Ewens might have half the increase which was accordingly rendered unto him by the said negro and the other half reserved for his own benefit: And whereas the said negro having a young child of a negro woman belonging to Lt. Robert Sheppard which he desired be taught and exercised in the church of England, by reason whereof he, the said negro did for his said child purchase its freedom of Lt. Sheppard with the good liking and consent of Tho. Goodman, Ewens' overseer, as by the deposition of the said Sheppard and Ewens appeareth, the court hath therefore ordered that the child shall be free from the said Ewens or his assigns and to be and remain at the disposing and education of the said Gowen and the child's godfather who undertaketh to see it brought up in the Christian religion as aforesaid."

April 1641

John Gowen indentures his son Mihill to Christopher Stafford. Gowen knew how to maneuver through the English legal system. This one indenture would begin the process of guaranteeing the freedoms of some of the first Africans in Virginia.

[October 25, 1657—From a legal statement by Anne Barnhouse: "Bee itt known unto all Christian people that whereas Mihill Gowen Negro of late servant to my Brother Xopher Stafford deced by his last will & Testament bearing Date the 18 of Jan 1654 had his freedom given unto him after the expiration of 4 years' service unto my uncle Robert Stafford. *Therefore know all whom itt may concern that I Anne Barnehouse for divers good couses mee hereunto moving do absolutely quitt & discharge the sd Mihill Gowen from any service & for ever sett him free from any claim of service either by mee or any one my behalf as any part or parcell of my Estate that may be claimed by mee the said Amy Barnhouse my heyres Exers Admrs or Assignes as witness my hand this 25 Oct 1657. Amy (AB) Barnhouse. Bee itt knowne unto all Xcian people that I Ame Barnehouse of Martins hundred widdow for divers good causes & consideracons mee hereunto moving hath given unto Mihill Gowen Negro he being att this time servant unto Robert Stafford a Male child borne the 25 August 1655 of the body of my Negro Prossa being baptized by Mr. Edward Johnson 2 Sept 1655 & named William & I the said Amy Barnhouse doth bind my selfe my heyres Exer Admr & Ass never to trouble or molest the*

said Mihill Gowin or his sone William or demand any service of
the said Mihill or his said son William. In witness where of I have
caused this to be made & done I hereunto sett my hand & Seale
this present 16 Sept 1655. Amy (AB) Barnhouse."]

March 1643

Changes in taxes/tithables: "All males, both European and Negro,
of the age of 16 yrs and older and all Negro Females 16 years of
age and older shall be taxable."

September 30, 1643

William Ewens recertifies his original patent from September 1619:
"1,100 acs., James City Co., Page 904." His headrights include
Michael, a Negro; Katherine, his wife; John Grasheare, a Negro;
and Mathew, a Negro. Note: John Grasheare is the same person as
the John Gowen mentioned earlier. Those people noted here were
not recorded in the population censuses of 1623, 1624, or 1625.

February 1645

Changes in taxes/tithables: "All men between the ages of 16 and
60, and all African men and women shall be tithable."

May 1645

Emmanuel Driggers indentures his adoptive daughter Jane, at the
age of one year old, to be bound to Captain Francis Pott to serve
him until the age of thirty-one. Emmanuel Driggers also "bought
and paid Capt. Robert Shepard for the child." Note: A slave would
not be allowed to indenture his child.

May 27, 1645

According to the records, Emmanuel Driggers, a "slave" of Francis
Pott on his plantation in Magotha Bay, Northampton County,
Virginia, purchases a cow and calf from Pott and records the sale

in the Northampton County Court. However, a true slave would not likely be allowed to own, buy, and sell livestock at his ease. Therefore, the term "slave" is not always accurate as to today's definition or perception of slavery. In addition, the following is a list of additional transactions where Driggers demonstrated freedom that a slave would not have:

- Emmanuel Driggers and his wife, Frances, are assigned to Stephen Charlton in 1649 to pay Pott's debt to Charlton. On December 30, 1652, Driggers's former masters, Francis Pott and Stephen Charlton, clarify the status of the cattle he and Bashaw Farnando acquired while they were his servants (slaves), declaring that "ye said cattle, etc. are ye proper goods of the sd Negroes."
- On September 16, 1661, Emmanuel Driggers sells a black heifer to Joan, daughter of Peter George.
- By October 1, 1661, Driggers has married his second wife, Elizabeth, with whom he made a deed of jointure in which he gave her a three-year-old mare and its increase.
- Emmanuel Driggers is also called "Manuell Rodriges" in 1660–1663 when he is head of a Northampton County household, taxable on three tithes.
- In 1665 Emmanuel Driggers leases 245 acres for ninety-nine years from his former master, William Kendall, and in 1672 assigns the unexpired part of the lease to John Waterson.

June 1650
John Upton renews his patent using Anthony and Mary Johnson as headrights from his original patent, July 7, 1635.

July 1651
Anthony Johnson, a free Negro, patents 250 acres in Northampton County.

May 24, 1652

When Jane Driggers is eight years old, her adoptive father, Emmanuel Driggers, pays Captain Pott for her freedom. Jane is the natural daughter of Margaret Cornish and Robert Sweat of Robert Sheppard's plantation. (The connection between Margaret Cornish, Jane Sweat's biological mother, and Emmanuel Driggers was Driggers's wife, Frances. Margaret and Frances were together at Bennett's plantation/Warrasquarake in the List of the Living and Dead in 1623.

1655–1659

In 1655 the court records a debt of 1,373 pounds that Charlton owes "her Negro man for his share of the Crop." The inventory of the estate of Bridgett Charlton shows "the two Negro crops in 1658 was 1,220 pounds of tobacco. The two Negro crops in 1659 is 2,155 pounds, and the Negro Man's crop in 1660 was 1,380."

March 1655

Anthony Johnson goes to court to retain his servant John Casor.

January 1656

Elizabeth Key, a Negro girl, sues for her freedom. Her father is a white man, and her mother a Negro. Key wins her freedom with the status of her free European father and the notation of her baptism.

1659

Mary Ewens, widow of William Ewens, inherits the Africans Michael, Katherine, and their five children—Rebecca, Frances, Amos, Susanna, and the youngest child unnamed—residing at the College Land, Surry County.

1662

A sizable community of free Africans is paying their own tithes and living in their own homes in Surry County, Northampton County, Virginia.

December 1662

The Virginia General Assembly declares that all children born in this land shall be held in bond or free only according to the mother's condition.

1667

Virginia is actively involved in slavery.

April 1667

Emmanuel Cambew/Cambo/Cambow, an African man, patents fifty acres.

September 1667

Legislation supporting slavery is further ensured when a law is enacted stating that a person's baptismal status can no longer alter a person's bondage or freedom.

Afterword

Preface

By the time the Africans arrived in Virginia in 1619, the Company had already begun to fracture, with the unsettled death of Lord De La Warr and the warrant by Sandys for the treasurer. The game of chess between Warwick and Sandys had already begun. Unfortunately for the Africans, their lives were subsumed under a cover-up, caught in an illusion, robbed of their true place in history.

Chapter 1—*Massacre on the Kingdom of Ndongo*

With the thorough work of Linda Heywood and John Thornton, discussed in their many books—especially *Central Africans, Atlantic Creoles, and the Foundation of the Americas 1585–1660*—the choice was made not to rehash sixteenth- and seventeenth-century African history. Their work is untouchable, and readers are encouraged to seek it out.

Chapter 2—*From the Port of Luanda*
The *San Juan Bautista* was in the port of Luanda to purchase slaves in conjunction with the contract of Antonio Fernandes Delvas, a Lisbon banker. During the years of 1615 to 1622, Delvas was allowed to ship between thirty-five hundred and five thousand Africans per year from Luanda, Angola. For the exclusive right of importing slaves, Delvas paid the Spanish Crown 115,000 ducats annually.[1] Under Delvas's contract, thirty-six slavers would sail from Luanda. Of the thirty-six, six sailed to Veracruz, New Spain. Of the six, only one would report a piracy in the Bay of Campeche.

Chapter 3—*A Light in the Darkness*
Because of a comment that John Dutton made, many historians believe the *Treasurer* never returned to Virginia with Africans in early 1620.[2] Dutton's statement—"*wee met with the Treasurer so weather beaten and tourne, as never likely to be put to sea againe*"—needs to be noted as personal opinion and not fact. His statement does not give certainty to a claim that the *Treasurer* was too far gone to be refit for one last mission. Governor Butler, who was little more than Warwick's puppet, knew the refitting of the *Treasurer* would be difficult, especially enough to withstand a winter's journey. But more significantly the *Treasurer* was being used for "other secret reasons, whereby it was conceived the Governor could not choose, but hold her altogether improper for the employment."[3] The *Treasurer* would provide passage for the Africans back to Virginia, further camouflaging the events of the *San Juan Bautista* piracy scandal. Governor Butler was also hoping to rid Bermuda of any type of retaliation from the Spanish government for being involved with the event. By March 1620, when the census was taken, the number of Africans in Virginia had gone from fourteen to thirty-two.

Chapter 4—*Political Wrangling*

When the *White Lion* sailed from Virginia in early October 1619, Captain Jope definitely would have sailed back to Bermuda. Whether he would have been delivering the cover-up plan from Warwick's allies in Virginia or just giving the governor an update on the concerns in Virginia is questionable. Without doubt, at a minimum, Jope would have collected the four crew members and the two Africans who were previously detained in Bermuda.

Governor Nathaniel Butler wrote in a letter to Warwick in October 1620 how the first fourteen Africans Kendall purchased from Kirby were originally from Captain Jope.[4] Butler closed the letter, "I humbly thank your Lordship for my two." The questions must be asked: Were these "two" Africans received in trade for the governor's loyalty? Or was it part of a bribe for removing the Africans from Bermuda? One thing this notation does indicate is there were definitely additional communications of instruction between Warwick and Butler regarding the Africans' relocation.

Chapter 5—*The Slaver: The* San Juan Bautista

The origins of the *San Juan Bautista* are significant to this account. The specifications of the *San Juan Bautista* allow us to determine whether the two English corsairs were hunting slavers in the Bay of Campeche or a Spanish galleon possibly carrying jewels from the mines in New Spain back to the Spanish mainland. Unless the two English captains knew there were slaves in the underbelly of the *San Juan Bautista* prior to pirating her, they surely were not looking for slaves to take back to Virginia or Bermuda. If they were looking for slaves, they would have targeted a slaver. In Engel Sluiter's original translation of the receipt of Mendez de Acuña's Africans, he notes the ship as the *Sao Joao Bautista*. Further, in the same research, Sluiter noted that he had changed the name of the ship and the captain to Portuguese. The translation has been represented in both Engel Sluiter's research notes and the *William and Mary Quarterly*. Specifications and a reproduction of the *San Juan Bautista* are at the San Juan Bautista Museum in Ishinomaki, Japan.

Chapter 6—*Two English Corsairs*

Captain Mendez de Acuña of the *San Juan Bautista* on August 30, 1619, described the "English corsairs" appropriately; history has proven him correct. Corsairs were warships similar to the Spanish galleon type. Manned with arms to defend treasure, they made excellent pirate ships. Sleek and slender, they were faster than the merchant cargo ships.

Chapter 7—*Identifying Those Involved*

Captain John Jope

According to the genealogy completed by Major Hugh Jope, John Colyn Jope was a Calvinist reverend who gained the *White Lion* from a member of his congregation and refurbished the ship over a ten-year period before heading out on his maiden voyage in 1619.[5] However, additional research shows the greater possibility of a different John Jope;[6] a seasoned merchant and part-time privateer out of the port of Plymouth, Devon, was quite possibly the true Captain John Jope who participated in the battle of the *Bautista* in the summer of 1619. Captain John Jope of Plymouth, Devon, was known to carry multiple marques—one being a Flemish-Dutch marque from Prince Maurice of Orange. Both John Jopes descend from the same Jope ancestor.

In 1620 John Jope presented Robert Bennett's lineage for the Visitation of the County of Cornwall with the note: "John Jope for Rob. Bennett."[7] This visitation notation bolsters the notion of the *White Lion*'s return in May 1622, placing Margaret at Bennett's plantation.[8]

Earl of Warwick

The following is a list of the Earl of Warwick's allies in Virginia, Bermuda, and England involved in the cover-up of the events surrounding the *San Juan Bautista* piracy.

- Nathaniel Rich—His first cousin, responsible for Warwick's legal dealings.
- Samuel Argall—Rich's partner in the *Treasurer.*
- Captain Daniel Elfrith—Captained the *Treasurer* and would later claim Providence Island in Warwick's name.
- Robert Rich—The younger brother of Nathaniel Rich, a Bermuda ally.
- Governor Nathaniel Butler—Provided letters informing Rich of promises to be fulfilled.
- John Dutton—Sent letters to Warwick; sister was connected to the Rich family.
- Governor George Yeardley—Protected both the *White Lion* and the *Treasurer*. Nominated Marmaduke Rayner to survey the lower lands of Carolina in January 1619/20.
- John Pory—Didn't mention the Africans in his letter dated September 30, 1619, to Sir Dudley Charlton, which Marmaduke Rayner carried for Pory. Pory lived in Jamestown, probably with his kin, the Yeardleys. Therefore, time must have been spent in the presence of Governor Yeardley. The *White Lion* spent as many as forty-five days within the settlement.
- Captain William Pierce—One of two captains who reported back to Yeardley only seeing the *Treasurer*'s sails in the distance leaving Point Comfort.
- Captain William Ewens—One of two captains who reported back to Yeardley only seeing the *Treasurer*'s sails in the distance leaving Point Comfort. Captained several of Warwick's ships for the Company.

- Edward Bennett—Fellow Puritan leader and Company investor.
- Commander William Tucker—Did not detain the *Treasurer* or arrest her captain upon her arrival with the pirated Africans.
- Maurice Thompson—Warwick's operations manager in Virginia was at Point Comfort upon the *Treasurer*'s arrival in 1619.
- Captain Francis West—Testified in 1623 on behalf of Warwick and returned to Virginia via New England with John Pedro from Leez Priory, Warwick's Felsted estate.

Marmaduke Rayner
In Rolfe's letter dated January 1620, Marmaduke Rayner is portrayed as an unfamiliar pilot. To further prove the skewed narrative of the Africans' arrival, in a written testimony, Marmaduke noted that he had frequented Virginia and lived there some sixteen months.[9]

Captain William Tucker
By 1623, when Captain Tucker brought his wife to Virginia, she arrived on the *George* along with her three other siblings, William, George, and Paule. By 1623, their older brother Maurice had lived and worked with Captain Tucker for at least five years.[10]

- Tucker, Mary, 1623 voyage, wife of Captain William Tucker, muster at Elizabeth City[11]
- Thompson, William, 1623 voyage, age seventeen at muster at Elizabeth City under Captain William Tucker[12]
- Tompson, George, 1623 voyage, age seventeen at muster at Elizabeth City under Captain William Tucker[13]
- Tompson, Paule, 1623 voyage, age fourteen at muster at Elizabeth City under Captain William Tucker[14]

Deputy Governor Miles Kendall
Historian John Burk wrote in 1804,

> In the latter time that captain Kendall was deputy gover-
> nor, there arrived a man of war with a commission from
> the prince of Orange, by virtue where he had taken certain
> negroes in the West Indies; and being in great extremity for
> want of water and victuals, and forbid by captain Kendall to
> come into any of the said harbors, he gave Kendall notice,
> he had fourteen negroes on board, which he should be forced
> to cast overboard for want of victuals, and rather desired to
> bestow them on captain Kendall, for any small consideration
> which he should be pleased to bestow on them.[15]

Whether Kendall purchased the fourteen Africans directly
from the *White Lion* or from Kirby remains somewhat of a
mystery. In his letter to Warwick, Kendall said, "he found them
floating on the seas." The *White Lion*'s captain said, "he would
throw them overboard." Which version represents the truth, we
may never know. One thing we do know is fourteen of the *San
Juan Bautista*'s Africans were brought to Bermuda the middle of
August 1619.

Chapter 8—*Dissecting the Original Count*
The total number of Africans whom Captain Manuel Mendez de
Acuña reported stolen in Veracruz was sixty. The number reported
in John Rolfe's letter to the Virginia Company of London was
very much ambiguous: "20, & odd." Evidence from the Bermuda
records notes the *Treasurer*'s return in early 1620 under "secret
reasons." This was before the March census of 1620 and more
than likely at the same time that Rolfe's January 1620 letter was
written. Rolfe probably wrote "20, & odd" because he was yet to

know for certain the specific amount who would be returning on the *Treasurer* from Bermuda.

Beyond the information available in this volume, no further details are yet available about Virginia's thirty-two Africans.

Chapter 10—*The Africans*

In 1619 the Ndongo king lived outside of the Ndongo capital of Kabasa, reportedly in or near the city of Pungo. The associations with the names of Pungoteague and Matchepungo, both areas in Northampton County where many of the early Africans resided, are significant. The areas were quite possibly named as a gesture to the Africans' origin.

Frances Driggers

The first single/unwed African mother in Virginia who raised "her child" on her own.

Peter George

Between 1645 and 1677, Peter George was located in Northampton County, Virginia, where he was indentured to several of the large plantation owners. Peter George's family, like his parents, Emmanuel and Frances Driggers, can be followed through the Potts, Harmer, Littleton, and Pigot families of Northampton County. The connections between these families are remarkable.

Margaret Cornish

She may have been the Negro Margaret recorded in 1636 as a headright in the three-thousand-acre patent of Lieutenant Colonel Richard Cocke. If this Margaret is indeed Margaret Cornish, she would have been transferred to Lieutenant Robert Sheppard prior to October 1640. She remained with Sheppard until 1653 at the time of his death. The same year, Margaret was listed with her youngest son, Anthony, as headrights in the patent of Colonel Rawleigh Traverse.[16] There is a noticeable trail of militiamen to whom Margaret was indentured or with whom she was associated. The three listed here were in addition to Captain Charles Barham, a justice and sheriff for Surry County she worked for in 1666 when she witnessed an indenture for a young English girl.[17]

The following were Margaret Cornish and Robert Sweat's children:

- **Robert Cornish Sweat** (b. 1640–1641)—Robert, the eldest child of Margaret Cornish and Robert Sweat, and the basis for the October 1640 ruling for a Negro woman's punishment of fornication with an Englishman.
- **William Sweat** (b. 1642)—The second child of Margaret Cornish and Robert Sweat. William was tithable in the residence of Thomas Binns and would later be tithable under Binns's son-in-law, Francis Mason. Mason was a major in the Surry County Militia as well as a justice and a burgess in 1692.

William Sweat/Swett's children were probably as follows:

- *Robert*, b. ca. 1670 and taxable in Francis Mason's household from 1686 to 1693. By 1695 he was tithable in his own household.[18] Robert married a woman named Margaret, whom they called Margaret the younger. With Margaret, Robert had one child, Cornish Sweat, b. ca. 1690. Robert died at age twenty-six. Both his father, William Sweat, and uncle Anthony Cornish were security for his widow, Margaret Swett, on the estate of Robert Sweat in 1696.[19] Soon after, Margaret Swett married John Tann (Kicotan).
- *William Jr.*, b. ca. 1676, was taxable in Surry County from 1698 to 1703 in William Sweat Sr.'s household.

- *Eve*, b. ca. 1678, may have been the unnamed mulatto daughter of William Sweat whom the court ruled was not tithable in 1694.

- **Jane Sweat** (b. 1644)—The daughter of Robert Sweat and Margaret Cornish, adopted by Frances and Emmanuel Driggers of Northampton County in 1645 at the age of one. Driggers paid her mother's master, Lieutenant Robert Sheppard, for her release. It appears that Robert Sweat, her father, was killed or died shortly after the third and final Powhatan uprising of 1644. The area where they lived, known as Sweat House Swamp, was hit hard. In 1643 Margaret Cornish, Jane's biological mother, became taxable. With the loss of her father, Margaret's pregnancy with a boy was more than enough reason for Jane's adoption. If Robert Sweat, Jane's father, did die in 1644, the courts quite possibly required the girl to be bound out. By 1652, Emmanuel Driggers had paid Francis Pott for the release of Jane after only seven years. Before 1663 Jane Driggus had a daughter with Denham Landrum, an Irishman, and was punished for fornication with thirty lashes (history repeating itself). By 1663 Jane married John Gossall. In less than three years, Gossall was dead. Jane then married William Harman, an African man. In addition to Sarah Landrum, her first daughter, Jane had two more children, whom she named after her adoptive parents, a daughter, Frances, and a son, Manuel.

Frances would have a child with Samuel Johnson prior to 1684, when an order was entered for the sheriff to hold Johnson until he posted bond for the child.[20] In May 1688 Frances Harman was named as a "servant" to Colonel Custis.[21] Three years later, in January 1691, Frances Harman was presented to the grand jury for having a bastard child.[22]

The following year, Frances acknowledged a bastard child and received twenty lashes on her naked shoulders.[23]

- **Anthony** (b. 1645)—Anthony Cornish was probably born after his father's death in 1644–1645. Anthony was given his mother's surname of Cornish. In 1654, at age nine, Anthony was used as a headright along with his mother.[24] After he reached the age of sixteen, he was tithable with his mother, Margaret, in Lawnes Creek Parish, Surry County, where he lived until 1673—at which point Margaret was no longer tithable and disappeared from the record.

  Anthony first married Katherine Cornish, an English-woman, with whom he had at least two children. The first, Robert Cornish, was born about 1677 and listed in 1693 and 1694 in the father's household in Surry County.[25] The second, a daughter named Elizabeth, was born about 1685. Elizabeth was taxable in 1701 in the household of Anthony Cornish's neighbor, James Ely.[26] By 1698 Anthony's first wife, Katherine, must have died when he took a second wife, Margaret Shaw, who became Margaret Cornish, listed as taxable in the household of John Hencock of Lawnes Creek Parish in 1703.[27]

The following are descendants of the Cornish/Sweat union. Notice the same names used over and over.

- William Sweat, b. 1700
- Robert Sweat, b. 1707
- Margaret Sweat, b. 1728
- Sarah Sweat, b. 1730
- William Sweat, b. 1730
- William Sweat, b. 1732
- Thomas Sweat, b. 1738

- Anthony Sweat, b. 1741
- Anthony Sweat, b. 1757
- William Sweat, b. 1760
- James Sweat, b. 1765[28]

John Gowen/Gruyere/Goin

Presumably John was one of the two Africans noted in the "depths of Somerset" with the *White Lion* crew returning from Virginia. John left England in July 1622 on the *James*. Upon his arrival in Virginia, he was taken to Ewens's plantation.[29] The *James* was owned by Warwick and undoubtedly was in contact with John Jope, the captain of the *White Lion*. John Gowen did live at William Ewens's plantation. According to Hashaw, John was named on a ship list as part of the crew of the *White Lion* as late as 1626.[30] In 1627 a Negro arrived at the Ewens plantation on the south side of the James River known as the College Land by way of the *Saker*.[31] The master of the *Saker* was none other than Marmaduke Rayner, the pilot of the *White Lion*.[32] There are two possibilities of who this African was: either John Gowen, returning to Ewens's plantation, or Mathew (Matthew), another African listed at Ewens's plantation from 1628 to 1643.

John's eldest son, Mihill Gowen (b. 1635), had four sons.

- William, b. August 1655, the son of Prossa, was baptized September 25, 1655.[33] William Gowen received a grant of land in Charles City County on April 20, 1687.[34]
- Daniel, b. ca. 1657, received a patent of one hundred acres in Kingston Parish, Gloucester County, on May 1, 1679.[35] In April 1698 Daniel received another fifty-two acres in Gloucester County.[36]
- Christopher, b. ca. 1658. He was living in Abingdon Parish, Gloucester County, with his wife, Ann Gowen, in January

1679 when their first child was born. Christopher and Ann may have had three children:

- Michal, b. January 1679[37]
- Phillip, b. ca. 1685
- Christopher[38]

• Thomas, b. ca. 1660, was living in Westmoreland County between 1693 and 1703 when he was involved in several court cases as both plaintiff and defendant.[39] He was called Thomas Goin of Westmoreland County on June 8, 1707, when he was granted 653 acres in Stafford County below the falls of the Potomac River.[40]

John's second son was Philip Gowen, b. 1649/50, mistakenly written "Philip Cowen, a Negro" when he petitioned the court for his freedom. His indenture to Amy Beazley was acknowledged in her last will and testament on April 9, 1664, stating, "Philip Gowen" would be free and receive three barrels of corn and a suit of clothes upon serving her cousin Humphrey Stafford for the last eight years of his indenture. Stafford sold the remaining years of Gowen's indenture to Charles Lucas, who was a schemer. Lucas forced Philip to acknowledge a twenty-year indenture to him in front of the court. In 1675, after Philip's eight years were completed he returned to court, at which time the court ruled Lucas's twenty-year indenture to be invalid and, further, that Philip should be rewarded his due. In 1675 Philip Gowen was a free man.

Undoubtedly, John Gowen indentured both of his sons to the Stafford family, showing a clear connection between the two brothers, Mihill and Philip.

Mathew
Mathew would have arrived on the *Treasurer* in March 1620 and was documented as living at Ewens's plantation, College Land, as

early as 1628 and remaining until at least 1643.[41] Very little documentation has been uncovered on Mathew. It's possible he was the unnamed African delivered to Ewens's plantation on the *Saker* in 1627.

Edward

Records indicate three generations of Edward:

- An *Edward* was listed at Ye Neck of Woods at Kingsmill between 1623 and 1625.
- *Edward Mozingo* (b. 1641–1644). On October 5, 1672, Edward completed his apprenticeship to Colonel John Walker.[42]
- *Edward Mozingo* (b. ca. 1664) married Sarah Grinstead about 1690. Mozingo is mentioned with his children Sarah and John in Sarah's mother's last will and testament.[43] Sarah was the sister of Ann Grimstead (Grinstead). The Grinstead family descended from the union of a mixed-race girl, Elizabeth Key, and her European husband, attorney John Grinstead. In July 1656, John Grinstead represented Key when she sued the colony for her freedom and won. This representation was prior to their marriage.

Edward, like most of the first Africans, indentured his son Edward to secure his future.

The 5th October 1672: Mozingos ordr for freedom Whereas it Appeareth by Divers Witneffes that had been Sworne and Examined that Edward Mozingo a negro man had been and was an apprentice by Indenture to Coll Jno Walker and that by Computation his terme of Servitude for Twenty Eight yeares is now Expired, The Court after a full hearing of the Matter In differrence Betweene the Said Edward Mozingo and Doctor

Stone who married Col Walkers Widdow, It is Adjudged by this Court that the Said Edward Mozingo be and Remain free to all Intents and purpofes by order of this Court.[44]

In Edward Mozingo's last will and testament, he transferred his two guns to his son. Edward directed his wife, Margaret, and two sons, John and Edward, to divide the remainder of his personal estate equally. His wife received her dower, and at her death, John and Edward were to divide the land equally. His will was probated May 7, 1712.[45]

Angela/Angelo

Angela arrived on the *Treasurer*. She was given to—or purchased by—Lieutenant William Pierce. Debate remains strong among historians as to the year of her arrival. It's possible that Angela departed the *Treasurer* in 1619 at Point Comfort and was given to Pierce for insurance of the *Treasurer*'s safe departure. However, Angela might also have been among the Africans brought back to Virginia on the *Treasurer* prior to March 1620 and listed among the thirty-two Africans in the 1620 census. John Rolfe, William Pierce's son-in-law, wrote the first letter to the Virginia Company of London mentioning the Africans' arrival five months after the *White Lion* had anchored, and most likely after he was made aware of the *Treasurer*'s second coming in early 1620—plenty of time for Warwick's allies to scramble together to set in place a cover-up story for Warwick's ties to the illegal affair. On December 31, 1619, Pierce's patent for 650 acres on Mulberry Island was recorded. Therefore, upon her arrival in early 1620, Angela would have been taken to Pierce's plantation. In 1621, with the arrival of Governor Wyatt, Pierce was made captain of the militia, and he returned to Jamestown. More probably, Angela went to Jamestown after the Native uprising of March 1622, when all of Pierce's Mulberry Island Plantation was removed to Jamestown.

WILLIAM PEIRCE, 2,100 acs. beg. at the mouth of a cr. near the now dwelling house of sd. Peirce, 650 acs. by patent to him dated 31 Dec. 1619, & 1,450 acs. due for the adventure of 29 persons. Re-patented Dec. 16, 1643, Page 927.[46]

Antonio/Anthony Johnson
Major Hugh Jope cited the inquiry testimony identifying Antonio as the Angolan who testified how the Africans were taken from the *San Juan Bautista* slaver in the summer of 1619.[47] Anthony Johnson with his wife, Mary, had one of the most successful livestock monopolies in Northampton County.

Toney King
"On February 8, 1677 will of King Tony, Negro was proved."[48] From the following portion of the will, in addition to his daughter, Sarah, we can confirm the names of his wife and granddaughter. There were three generations of women named Sarah.

> I King Tony Negro give unto my grandchild Sarah Driggus the first cow calfe either of my Cowes shall bring . . . my steere & one hog bee spent by my Executrix and loving wife at my Funeral when I depart this life. All the rest of my estate whatsoever unto my loving wife Sarah. 6 February 1677. witnesses: Peter x George, Daniel x Webb.[49]

Emmanuel Driggers
Emmanuel and his wife, Frances, should be known as the earliest freedom fighters in North America. Their two adoptive daughters are the best representation of this assertion. Two girls, Elizabeth and Jane, found themselves without fathers. In 1645 Emmanuel and Frances Driggers adopted the girls and immediately bound them to their master, Captain Francis Pott. This one act guaranteed

the two girls an end date to their service and their eventual freedom. It also allowed for the option of purchasing the debt owed to the children's master, which could be paid for their release. This option was exercised in 1652, when Jane Driggers was released from her contract.

Progression from Pott to Pigot. In 1635, several of the 1619 Africans were indentured to Captain Francis Pott. Living adjacent to Pott was Charles Harmer, who, in 1635, patented 1,050 acres. Among Harmer's headrights are eight Africans: Alexander, Anthony, Sebastian, Polonia, Jane, Palatia, Cassanga, and John. They are not listed as slaves but indentured headrights from their transport. Sometime after March 1640 Captain Nathaniel Littleton married Ann Southey Harmer, the widow of Charles Harmer.[50] According to Ann Littleton's will,[51] where Captain Francis Pott is named a trustee, she distributes the indentured servants among her descendants. Sebastian, John, and Anthony (Tony) are among them, who were Harmer's headrights in 1635.

Then in 1656 Edward Littleton, the eldest son of Captain Nathaniel Littleton, received his inheritance: the Magotha Bay Plantation, along with all the livestock, servants, and other property. Upon the passing of Edward's first wife, he married Frances Robins in March 1660. After Edward Littleton's death, Frances Robins Littleton married Colonel Francis Pigot. Into the 1670s and 1680s most of Peter George's immediate family remained indentured to Pigot.

Peter George sued for his livestock from his former master.

Case between Peter George Negro plaintiff, and Elizabeth Candlin, said defendant, widow and administrator of her husband Robert Candlin, deceased, refer to jury. Judgement found for plaintiff . . . defendant deliver to the said plaintiff the cattle and hogs with their increase.[52]

Chapter 11—*Slavery vs. Servitude*

In 1623 the Somers Isle Company of Bermuda established the first act toward instituting slavery—the Act of Insolence—"to restrain the insolence of the Negroes." The act forbade blacks from buying, selling, bartering, or exchanging tobacco or any other produce for goods without consent of their master. Such laws would take a little while longer coming to Virginia, not long after the first Africans' ambiguous status would be resolved in 1628. With the realization of the Africans' "new" status of indentured, the following laws were enacted against the Africans:[53]

October 1629

All those that worke in the ground of quality or condition whatsoever, shall pay tithes to the minister.

1640

England becomes more involved and accepting of the transport and sales of slaves into the English colonies. Laws begin to reflect a distinct downturn for the Africans.

January 1640

All people "except negroes" were to be provided with firearms and ammunition.

1641

Massachusetts passes its "Body of Liberties," giving legal sanction to certain types of slavery:

There shall never be any bond slaverie, villinage or captivitie amongst us unless it be lawfull captives taken in just warres, and such strangers as willingly selle themselves or are sold to us. And these shall have all the liberties and Christian usages which the law of God established in Israell concerning such persons doeth morally require. This exempts none from servitude who shall be judged thereto by Authoritie.

The reference to "strangers" is from Leviticus 25:39–55 and explains that they could be ruled and sold as slaves. In the Massachusetts Colony, the Puritans would use the term "strangers" to imply Africans and Native Americans. Even though the "Body of Liberties" excluded many forms of slavery, it did recognize four to be legitimate:

- Slaves who were legally obtained as captives of war
- Those who sold themselves into slavery
- Those who were purchased elsewhere as slaves and brought into the colony
- Those sentenced to slavery as punishment through the governing authority

March 1643

Whereas many great abuses and much detriment have been found to arise both against the law of God and likewise to the service of manye masters of families in the collony occasioned through secret marriages of servants, their masters and mistresses being not any ways made privy thereto, as also by committing of fornication, for preventing the like abuses hereafter, Be it enacted and confirmed by this Grand Assembly that what man servant soever hath since January 1640 or hereafter shall secretly marry with any mayd or woman servant without the consent of her master or mistress if she be a widow, he or they so offending shall in the first place serve out his or their tyme or tymes with his or their masters or mistresses, and after shall serve his or their master or mistress one compleat year more for such offence committed, And the mayd or woman servant so marrying without consent as aforesaid shall for such her offence double the tyme of service with her master and mistress, And a freeman so offending shall give satisfaction to the master or mistress by doubling the value of the service and pay a ffine of five hundred pounds of tobacco to the parish where such offence shall be omitted. . . .

Whereas complaints are at every quarter court exhibitted against divers persons who entertain and enter into covenants with runaway servants and freemen who have formerly hired themselves to others to the great prejudice if not the utter undoeing of divers porr men, thereby also encourageing servants to runn from their masters and obscure themselves in some remote plantations, Upon consideration had for the future preventing of the like injurious and unjust dealings, Be it enacted and confirmed that what person or persons soever shall entertain any person as hireling, or sharer or upon any other conditions for one whole yeare without certificate from the commander or any one commissioner of the place, that he or she is free from any ingagement of service, The person so hireing without such certificate as aforesaid, shall for every night that he or she entertaineth any servant either as hireling or otherwise, fforfeit to the master or mistris of the said servant twenty pounds of tobacco.

Whereas there are divers loytering runaways in the collony who very often absent themselves from their masters service, And sometimes in two or three monthes cannot be found, whereby their said masters are at great charge in finding them, And many times even to the loss of their year's labour before they be had, Be it therefore enacted and confirmed that all runaways that shall absent themselves from *their said masters service shall be lyable to make satisfaction by service at the end of their tymes by indenture double the tyme of service soe neglected, And in some cases more if the comissioners for the place appointed shall find it requisite and convenient. And if such runaways shall be found to transgresse the second time or oftener (if it shall be duely proved against them) that then they shall be branded in the cheek with the letter R. and passe under the statute of incorrigible rogues.*

March 1658

Whereas divers ill disposed persons do secretly and covertly trade and truck with other mens' servants and aprentices which tendeth to the great injurie of masters of ffamilies their servants being thereby induced and invited to purloine and imbezill the goods of their said masters, Bee it therefore enacted for redresse of the like disorders and abuses hereafter that what person or persons shall buy, sell, trade or truck with any servant, for any comoditie whatsoever without lycence or consent of the master of any such servant hee or they so offending against the premises shall suffer one monthes imprisonment without bail or mainprize and also shall forfeite and restore to the master of the said servant fower times the value of the things so bought, sold, trucked or traded for.

March 1661

Bee it enacted That in case any English servant shall run away in company with any negroes who are incapable of making satisfation by addition of time, Bee it enacted that the English so running away in company with them shall serve for the time of the said negroes absence as they are to do for their owne by a former act.

March 1661

Whereas the barbarous usage of some servants by cruell masters bring soe much scandall and infamy to the country in generall, that people who would willingly adventure themselves hither, are through feare thereof diverted, and by that meanes the supplies of particuler men and the well seating of his majesties country very much obstructed, Be it therefore enacted that every master shall provide for his servants compotent dyett, clothing and lodging, and that he shall not exceed the bounds of moderation in correcting them beyond the meritt of their offences; and that it shalbe lawfull for any servant giving notice to their masters (haveing just cause of complaint against them) for harsh and bad usage, or else of want of dyett or convenient necessaries to repaire to the next commissioner to make his or their complaint, and if the said commisioner shall find by just proofes that the said servants cause of complaint is just the said commissioner is hereby required to give order for the warning of such master to the next county court where the matter in difference shalbe determined, and the servant have remedy for his grievances.

December 1662

Whereas some doubts have arrisen whether children got by any Englishman upon a negro woman should be slave or ffree, Be it therefore enacted and declared by this present grand assembly, that all children borne in this country shalbe held bond or free only according to the condition of the mother, And that if any christian shall committ ffornication with a negro man or woman, hee or shee soe offending shall pay double the ffines imposed by the former act.

Afterword

September 1667

Whereas some doubts have risen whether children that are slaves by birth, and by the charity and piety of their owners made pertakers of the blessed sacrament of baptisme, should by vertue of their baptisme be made ffree; It is enacted and declared by this grand assembly, and the authority thereof, that the conferring of baptisme doth not alter the condition of the person as to his bondage or ffreedome; that diverse masters, ffreed from this doubt, may more carefully endeavour the propagation of christianity by permitting children, though slaves, or those of greater growth if capable to be admitted to that sacrament.

October 1670

Whereas it hath beene questioned whither Indians or negroes manumited, or otherwise free, could be capable of purchasing christian servants, It is enacted that noe negroe or Indian though baptised and enjoyned their owne ffreedome shall be capable of any such purchase of christians, but yet not debarred from buying any of their owne nation.

September 1672

Forasmuch as it hath beene manifested to this grand assembly that many negroes have lately beene, and now are out in rebellion in sundry parts of this country, and that noe meanes have yet beene found for the apprehension and suppression of them from whome many mischeifes of very dangerous consequence may arise to the country if either other negroes, Indians or servants should happen to fly forth and joyne with them; for the prevention of which, be it enacted by the governour, councell and burgesses of this grand assembly, and by the authority thereof, that if any negroe, molatto,

*Indian slave, or servant for life, runaway and shalbe persued
by the warrant or hue and crye, it shall and may be lawfull
for any person who shall endeavour to take them, upon the
resistance of such negroe, molatto, Indian slave, or servant
for life, to kill or wound him or them soe resisting; Provided
alwayes, and it is the true intent and meaning hereof, that
such negroe, molatto, Indian slave, or servant for life, be
named and described in the hue and crye which is alsoe to
be signed by the master or owner of the said runaway. And
if it happen that such negroe, molatto, Indian slave, or servant for life doe dye of any wound in such their resistance
received the master or owner of such shall receive satisfaction from the publique for his negroe, molatto, Indian slave,
or servant for life, soe killed or dyeing of such wounds; and
the person who shall kill or wound by virtue of any such
hugh and crye any such soe resisting in manner as aforesaid
shall not be questioned for the same, he forthwith giveing
notice thereof and returning the hue and crye or warrant to
the master or owner of him or them soe killed or wounded or
to the next justice of peace. . . .*

June 1680

*Whereas the frequent meeting of considerbale numbers of
negroe slaves under pretence of feasts and burialls is judged
of dangerous consequence; for prevention whereof for the
future, Bee it enacted by the kings most excellent majestie
by and with the consent of the generall assembly, and it is
hereby enacted by the authority foresaid, that from and after
the publication of this law, it shall not be lawfull for any
negroe or other slave to carry or arme himselfe with any
club, staffe, gunn, sword or any other weapon of defence
or offence, nor to goe or depart from of his masters ground*

without a certificate from his master, mistris or overseer and such permission not to be granted but upon perticuler and necessary occasions; and every negroe or slave soe offending not haveing a certificate as aforesaid shalbe sent to the next constable, who is hereby enjoyned and required to give the said negroe twenty lashes on his bare back well layd on, and soe sent home to his said master, mistris or overseer. And it is further enacted by the authority aforesaid that if any negroe or other slave shall presume to lift up his hand in opposition against any christian, shall for every such offence, upon due proofe made thereof by the oath of the party before a magistrate, have and receive thirty lashes on his bare back well laid on. And it is hereby further enacted by the authority aforesaid that if any negroe or other slave shall absent himself from his masters service and lye hid and lurking in obscure places, comitting injuries to the inhabitants, and shall resist any person or persons that shalby any lawfull authority by imployed to apprehend and take the said negroe, that then in case of such resistance, it shalbe lawfull for such person or persons to kill the said negroe or slave soe lying out and resisting, and that this law be once every six months published at the respective county courts and parish churches within this colony.

April 1691

Whereas many times negroes, mulattoes, and other slaves unlawfully absent themselves from their masters and mistresses service, and lie hid and lurk in obscure places killing hoggs and committing other injuries to the inhabitants of this dominion, for remedy whereof for the future, Be it enacted by their majesties lieutenant governour, councell and burgesses of this present general assembly, and the authoritie thereof, and it is hereby enacted, that in all such cases upon intelligence of any such negroes, mulattoes, or other slaves lying out, two of their majesties justices of the peace of that county, whereof one to be of the quorum, where such negroes, mulattoes or other slave shall be, shall be impowered and commanded, and are hereby impowered and commanded to issue out their warrants directed to the sherrife of the same county to apprehend such negroes, mulattoes, and other slaves, which said sherriffe is hereby likewise requred upon all such occasions to raise such and soe many forces from time to time as he shall think convenient and necessary for the effectual apprehending such negroes, mulattoes and other slaves, and in case any negroes, mulattoes or other slaves or slaves lying out as aforesaid shall resist, runaway, or refuse to deliver and surrender him or themselves to any person or persons that shall be by lawfull authority employed to apprehend and take such negroes, mulattoes or other slaves that in such cases it shall and may be lawfull for such person and persons to kill and distroy such negroes, mulattoes, and other slave or slaves by gunn or any otherwaise whatsoever. Provided that where any negroe or mulattoe slave or slaves shall be killed in pursuance of this act, the owner or owners of such negro or mulatto slave shall be paid for such negro or mulatto slave four thousand pounds of tobacco by the publique.

And for prevention of that abominable mixture and spurious issue which hereafter may encrease in this dominion, as well by negroes, mulattoes, and Indians intermarrying with English, or other white women, as by their unlawful accompanying with one another, Be it enacted by the authoritie aforesaid, and it is hereby enacted, that for the time to come, whatsoever English or other white man or woman being free shall intermarry with a negroe, mulatto, or Indian man or woman bond or free shall within three months after such marriage be banished and removed from this dominion forever, and that the justices of each respective countie within this dominion make it their perticular care that this act be put in effectuall execution. And be it further enacted by the authoritie aforesaid, and it is hereby enacted, That if any English woman being free shall have a bastard child by any negro or mulatto, she pay the sume of fifteen pounds sterling, within one moneth after such bastard child be born, to the Church wardens of the parish where she shall be delivered of such child, and in default of such payment she shall be taken into the possession of the said Church wardens and disposed of for five yeares, and the said fine of fifteen pounds, or whatever the woman shall be disposed of for, shall be paid, one third part to their majesties for and towards the support of the government and the contingent charges thereof, and one other third part to the use of the parish where the offence is committed, and the other third part to the informer, and that such bastard child be bound out as a servant by the said Church wardens untill he or she shall attaine the age of thirty yeares, and in case such English woman that shall have such bastard child be a servant, she shall be sold by the said church wardens, (after her time is expired that she ought by law to serve her master) for five yeares, and the money she shall be sold for divided as is before appointed, and the child to serve as aforesaid.

And forasmuch as great inconveniences may happen to this country by the setting of negroes and mulattoes free, by their either entertaining negro slaves from their masters service, or receiveing stolen goods, or being grown old bringing a charge upon the country; for prevention thereof, Be it enacted by the authority aforesaid, and it is hereby enacted, That no negro or mulatto be after the end of this present session of assembly set free by any person or persons whatsoever, unless such person or persons, their heires, executors or administrators pay for the transportation of such negro or negroes out of the countrey within six moneths after such setting them free, upon penalty of paying of tenn pounds sterling to the Church wardens of the parish where such person shall dwell with, which money, or so much thereof as shall be necessary, the said Church wardens are to cause the said negro or mulatto to be transported out of the countrey, and the remainder of the said money to imploy to the use of the poor of the parish.

By the turn of the century there were hundreds who descended from the 1619 Africans living free in Virginia. At every twist and turn, they faced the oppressive laws head on, fighting to provide for their families and maintain their "free" status and the enterprises they built. Many, regardless of the laws, married both Europeans and Native Americans, establishing Virginia's triracial community, called Malotto and sometimes later Melungeons as well. The struggles of the Melungeons weren't very different than those of the Africans.

Many descendants moved to areas more accepting of the free African and triracial communities. Like the Johnsons, some free African families moved north to Maryland where their grandson's plantation would reside decades later, named Angola. Others went south. Carter, Cumbo, Driggers, George, Gowen, and Sweat moved to Carolina—with entire communities relocating together.

The North Carolina counties of Bertie, Craven, Granville, Halifax, Herford, and Roberson seemed to tolerate them. However, Bladen County, North Carolina, was a different story: "The number of free negroes and mulattoes who infest that county and annoy its Inhabitants . . ."[54]

The colonial tax lists for Bladen County included the following mixed-race families. Braveboy, Carter, Chavis, Clark, Cox, Cumbo, Dimry, Doyal (Dial), Drake, Evans, Goin, Groom, Hammons, Overton, Oxendine, Perkins, Phillips, Russell, Skipper, Sweat, Sweeting, Walde, Wharton, Wilkins, and Wilson.[55]

Some of the same families were located in Roberson County just to the south, in the farmlands bordering South Carolina. In the 1790 and 1800 censuses, people represented as "other free" are traced back to persons recorded as "Negroes" in Virginia and North Carolina. They were the Branch, Braveboy, Brooks, Carter, Chavis, Cumbo, Dunn, Evans, Gowen, Hammond, Hogg, Oxendine, Revell, Roberts, Sweat, and Wilkins families.[56] Apparently more hospitable than Bladen County, in Roberson the Negroes were attending schools and churches, voting, and mustering along with the whites.[57]

Notes

1. *Goyen Family 2000—12 Dec Newsletter*.

2. January 20, 1620, Ives, *Rich Papers*, 141.

3. Lefroy, *History*, 158.

4. Ives, *Rich Papers*.

5. Hashaw, *Birth of Black America*.

6. John Jope's last will and testament, 1631, Devon County Records.

7. Vivian and Drake, *Visitation of the County of Cornwall*.

8. Kingsbury, *Records*, 3:639.

9. Neill, *Virginia Carolorum*.

10. Hotten, *Original Lists*, 201–65.

11. Ibid.

12. Ibid.

13. Ibid.

14. Ibid.

15. Burk, *History*, 326.

16. Nugent, *Cavaliers and Pioneers*, 581.

17. Heinegg, *Free African Americans*, 1:354–55.

18. MacDonald and Slatten, *Surry County Tithables*.

19. Haun, *Surry County*; Heinegg, *Free African Americans*, 2:1133.

20. Northampton County Records, Wills and Orders, March 2, 1684/5, 112.

21. Northampton County Records, Wills, Orders 1683-1689, LVA microfilm no. 27, 358.

22. Ibid., 148.

23. Ibid., 160.

24. Nugent, *Cavaliers and Pioneers*.

25. MacDonald and Slatten, *Surry County Tithables*.

26. "Surry County Tithables, 1698, 1699, 1700."

27. "Surry County Tithables, 1701, 1702, 1703."

28. Heinegg, *Free African Americans*.

29. Ferrar Papers, R.2 #400.

30. Admiralty Notes (PRO). A genealogy note on ancestry.com written by Tim Hashaw states that John Gowen was listed on the manifest as a *White Lion* crew member. If this is the young African John Gowen, he may have left with Captain Jope on the *White Lion* shortly after his arrival in July 1622 on the *James*. The *White Lion* was in Virginia around this time. Further research is necessary.

31. "William Ewens vs. the Saker," in Coldham, *English Adventurers and Immigrants*, 19.

32. Ibid.

33. York County Records, Deeds, Wills, and Orders.

34. Charles City County, Patents 7:58.

35. Gloucester County Records, Patents, 6, 679.

36. Ibid., 9, 147.

37. Gloucester County Records, Register, Abingdon Parish, 319.

38. Heinegg, *Free African Americans*, 1:544.

39. Westmoreland County Records.

40. Gray, *Virginia Northern Neck Land Grants*, 39.

41. Nugent, *Cavaliers and Pioneers*, 146.

42. McIlwaine, *Minutes of the Council*.

43. Westmoreland County Records, Cople Parish.

44. McIlwaine, *Minutes of the Council*, 75–76, 87.

45. Will of Edward Mozingo, July 30, 1711, Richmond County, Virginia, Will and Inventory, Vols. 1–3, 1699–1717.

46. Nugent, *Cavaliers and Pioneers*.

47. Hashaw, "Malungu."

48. Northampton County Records, Orders, Wills, Etc., 1674–1679, LVA microfilm no. 27, p. 239.

49. Ibid., 247.

50. Nugent, *Cavaliers and Pioneers*.

51. Turman and Lewis, "Will of Ann Littleton."

52. Northampton County Records, Wills and Orders, 1689–1698, book 13, LVA microfilm no. 27a.

53. "Slavery and the Law in Virginia."

54. Heinegg, *Free African Americans*, 1:24.

55. Ibid.

56. Ibid.

57. Ibid.

Appendix A:
Governors of Virginia, 1610–1645

Virginia Company of London's Governors:
1610–1624

1610–1618	Honorary Governor Thomas West, 3rd Baron De La Warr
1610	Deputy Governor Thomas Gates
1611	Deputy Governor George Percy
1611	Acting Governor Thomas Dale
1611–1613	Acting Governor Thomas Gates
1613–1616	Acting Governor Thomas Dale
1616–1617	Lieutenant Governor George Yeardley
1617–1619	Lieutenant Governor Samuel Argall
1619–1621	Governor George Yeardley
1621–1624	Governor Francis Wyatt

The Crown's Governors: 1624–1645

1624–1626	Governor Sir Francis Wyatt
1626–1627	Governor Sir George Yeardley

Appendix A: Governors of Virginia, 1610–1645

1627–1629	Acting Governor Francis West
1628–1639	Governor Sir John Harvey
1629–1630	Acting Governor John Pott
1635–1636	Acting Governor John West
1638–1639	Acting Governor George Reade
1639–1642	Governor Francis Wyatt
1642–1652	Governor William Berkeley
1644–1645	Acting Governor Richard Kemp

Appendix B:
Creation of Colonial
Counties

Corporation/Shire/ County	Year(s) Established	Created from
Accomack County (1)	1634, 1663	Eastern Shore
Charles City County (2)	1619, 1634	Original incorporation called Charles Cittie
Elizabeth City County (3)	1634	Kecoughtan
Gloucester County	1651	York County
Henrico	1617, 1619	Original incorporation
Henrico County (4)	1634	Henrico Cittie
Isle of Wight County (7a)	1634	Name changed from Warrosquyoake to Isle of Wight
James Cittie	1617, 1619	Original incorporation
James City County (5)	1634	James Cittie
Kecoughtan	1619	Original incorporation
Lancaster County	1651	Northumberland, York
New Kent County	1654	York County

(continues on next page)

Appendix B: Creation of Colonial Counties

Corporation/Shire/ County	Year(s) Established	Created from
Northampton County	1642	Accomack renamed
Northumberland County	1648	Geographic expansion into the Indian district (Wicocomico and Chickacoan tribes)
Rappahannock County	1656	Lancaster County
Stafford County	1664	Westmoreland
Surry County	1652	James City County
Warwick County	1643	Warwick River Shire
Warwick River Shire (6)	1634	Northern shore of James River became Warwick County
Warrosquyoake (7)	1634	Geographic expansion into the Indian district (Warrosquyoake tribe)
Westmoreland County	1653	Northumberland
York County (8)	1634	Also called Charles River Shire

Numbers in parentheses indicate Virginia's original shires (British term for counties).

Bibliography

Archive Abbreviations

Accomack County Records
Accomack County Records. Deeds, Wills, and Orders.

Boyd's Marriage Indexes
Birth, Marriage, Death, and Parish Records, Plymouth, Devon, England, 1538–1850.

Colonial Papers
Library of Virginia, Richmond, Virginia. Special Collections, Colonial Papers.

Devon County Records
Devon County, England, Birth, Marriage, Burial, and Death Records, including Parish Records.

Ferrar Papers
Ferrar Papers, Magdalene College, Cambridge, England, Microfilm Academic Publishers.

GCR
Virginia General Court Records.

Gloucester County Papers
Gloucester County Records. Deeds, Wills, Orders, Patents, and Parish Records.

LVA
Library of Virginia.

Manchester Papers
Manchester Papers, found in the Report of the Royal Commission on Historic Manuscripts, Great Britain Royal Commission on Historical Manuscripts Commission, PRO.

Northampton County Records
Northampton County Court Records. Deeds, Wills, Orders, and Court Minutes.

Privy Council
Acts of the Privy Council of England (1613–1631); HMSO, 1921–1964. Hathi Trust Digital Library.

PRO
Public Records Office.

Sluiter Collection
Engel Sluiter Historical Documents Collection. University of California–Berkeley, Bancroft Library.

Surry County Records
Surry County PRO. Deeds, Orders, Wills, and Patents.

Westmoreland County Records
Westmoreland County Records. Deeds, Orders, and Wills.

York County Records
York County PRO. Deeds, Orders, and Wills.

Other Archives and Primary Sources
Bermuda National Library, Hamilton, Bermuda.
Cornwall County, England. Birth, Marriage, Burial, and Death Records, including Parish Records.

Bibliography

Charles City County Records. Patents, Deeds, Orders, and Wills.

Elizabeth City County Records. Deeds, Orders, and Wills.

Gloucester County Register, Abingdon Parish.

John D. Rockefeller Jr. Library, Colonial Williamsburg Foundation.

National Archives and Records Administration, Washington, DC.

New Kent County Records. Deeds, Orders, and Wills.

Warwick County Public Records Office. Deeds, Orders, and Wills.

Books

Ballagh, James Curtis. *A History of Slavery in Virginia.* 1902; reprint, n.p.: Wentworth Press, 2016

Barbour, Phillip L., ed. *Travels and Works, Captain John Smith, President of Virginia and Admiral of New England, 1580–1631.* Volumes 1–3. Chapel Hill: University of North Carolina Press, 1986.

Bartolomé Benito, Fernando. *Don Diego Sarmiento de Acuña, conde de Gondomar.* Gijón: Trea, 2005.

Bell, John B. *Northampton County Virginia Tithables, 1662–1677.* Baltimore, MD: Heritage Books, 2008.

Bennett, Lerone, Jr. *Before the Mayflower: A History of Black America.* 6th revised edition. New York: Penguin Books, 1993.

Bernhard, Virginia. *Slaves and Slaveholders in Bermuda, 1616–1782.* Columbia: University of Missouri Press, 1999.

———. *A Tale of Two Colonies: What Really Happened in Virginia and Bermuda.* Columbia: University of Missouri Press, 2011.

Blair, E. H., and James Alexander Robertson, eds. *The Philippine Islands, 1493–1898.* Volume 18. *1617–1620.* Available at https://www.gutenberg.org/files/15564/15564-h/15564-h.htm.

Boddie, John Bennett. *Colonial Surry.* Richmond, VA: Dietz Press, 1948.

Boxer, C. R. *The Christian Century in Japan: 1549–1650.* Manchester: Carcanet Press, 1993.

Breen, T. H., and Stephen Innes. *"Myne Owne Ground": Race and Freedom on Virginia's Eastern Shore, 1640–1676.* New York: Oxford University Press, 2005.

Brown, Alexander. *The Genesis of the United States: A Narrative of the Movement in England, 1605–1616. . . .* 1890; reprint, n.p.: Forgotten Books, 2015.

Bibliography

Burk, John. *The History of Virginia from Its First Settlement to the Present Day.* Volume 1. Petersburg, VA: Printed for the author by Dickson and Pescud, 1804.

Chapman, Blanche Adams. *Marriages of Isle of Wight County, Virginia, 1628–1800.* Baltimore, MD: Clearfield, 2009.

Coldham, Peter Wilson. *English Adventurers and Emigrants, 1609–1660.* Baltimore, MD: Genealogical Publishing Company, 1984.

"Colonial Records of Virginia," 37–68. Richmond: Clement and Jones, 1874. https://ia600206.us.archive.org/31/items/colonialrecordso00 virg/colonialrecordso00virg.pdf.

Corbett, Julian Stafford. *Drake and the Tudor Navy, with a History of the Rise of England as a Maritime Power.* 1898; reprint, n.p.: Bibliolife, 2009.

Craven, Wesley Frank, *Dissolution of the Virginia Company: The Failure of a Colonial Experiment.* New York: Oxford University Press, 1932.

———. *The Virginia Company of London, 1606–1624.* Williamsburg, VA: Printed for Virginia 350th Anniversary Celebration Corporation, 1957.

Crozier, William Armstrong, ed. *Virginia Heraldica: Being a Registry of Virginia Gentry Entitled to Coat Armor, with Genealogical Notes of the Families.* New York: Genealogical Association, 1908.

Davis, Eliza Timberlake. *Surry County Records, Surry County, Virginia, 1652–1684.* Baltimore, MD: Genealogical Publishing Company, 1980.

Davis, Virginia Lee Hutcheson. *Jamestowne Ancestors, 1607–1699.* Baltimore, MD: Genealogical Publishing Company, 2009.

Deal, J. Douglas. R*ace and Class in Colonial Virginia: Indians, Englishmen, and Africans on the Eastern Shore during the Seventeenth Century.* New York: Garland, 1993.

Deetz, James. *Flowerdew Hundred: The Archaeology of a Virginia Plantation, 1619–1864.* Charlottesville: University of Virginia Press, 1993.

Dorman, John Fredrick. *Adventures of Purse and Person.* Baltimore, MD: Genealogical Publishing Company, 2004.

Duvall, Lindsay O. *Virginia Colonial Abstracts* 4, 2nd series, James City County, Virginia. Baltimore: Genealogical Publishing Co., 1961.

Feiling, Tom. *The Island That Disappeared: Old Providence and the Making of the Western World.* Brooklyn, NY: Melville House, 2018.

Finkelman, Paul. *Slavery in the Courtroom: An Annotated Bibliography of American Cases.* Washington, DC: Library of Congress, 1985.

Fiske, John. *The Historical Writings of John Fiske: Old Virginia and Her Neighbours.* Volumes 1–2. Boston: Houghton Mifflin Harcourt, 1897.

Foley, Louise Pledge Heath. *Early Virginia Families along the James River: James City County–Surry County.* Baltimore, MD: Genealogical Publishing Company, 1990.

———. *Early Virginia Families along the James River. Their Deep Roots and Tangled Branches. James City County–Surry County, Virginia.* Volume 3. Baltimore, MD: Clearfield, 2007.

Forgeng, Jeffrey. *Daily Life in Stuart England.* Westport, CT: Greenwood, 2007.

Gleanings of Major Robert Thompson (also known as Major Robert Thomson): Namesake of Thompson, CT. Thompson, CT: Thompson Historical Society, 2016.

Gonoi, Takashi. *Hasekura Tsunenaga* [The world and Japan: Tensho and Keicho missions to Europe, 16th–17th century] [Japanese: 支倉常長]. Tokyo: Yoshikawa Kobunkan, 2003.

Gray, Gertrude E. *Virginia Northern Neck Land Grants, 1694–1742.* Baltimore, MD: Clearfield, 1997.

Gregg, Alexander. *History of the Old Cheraws.* New York: Richardson and Company, 1867.

Hashaw, Tim. *The Birth of Black America: The First African Americans and the Pursuit of Freedom at Jamestown.* New York: Basic Books, 2007.

———. *Children of Perdition: Melungeons and the Struggle of Mixed America.* Macon, GA: Mercer University Press, 2006.

Hasler, P. W. *The History of Parliament: The House of Commons, 1558–1603.* London: Her Majesty's Stationery Office, 1981.

Hatch, Charles E., Jr. *The First Seventeen Years: Virginia, 1607–1624.* 2nd edition. Charlottesville: University Press of Virginia, 1995.

Haun, Weynette Parks. *Surry County, Virginia, Court Records.* Durham, NC: author, 1997.

Bibliography

Heinegg, Paul. *Free African Americans of North Carolina, Virginia, and South Carolina. From the Colonial Period to about 1820*. Volumes 1 and 2. 5th edition. Baltimore, MD: Clearfield, 2005.

Hening, William Waller. *The Statutes at Large; Being a Collection of All the Laws of Virginia, from the First Session of the Legislature in the Year 1619*. 13 volumes. Richmond, 1809–1823.

Heuman, Gad J., and James Walvin (eds.). *The Slavery Reader.* Routledge Readers in History. New York: Routledge, 2003.

Heywood, Linda M. *Central Africans and Cultural Transformation in the American Diaspora*. Cambridge: Cambridge University Press, 2001.

———. *Njinga of Angola: Africa's Warrior Queen*. Cambridge, MA: Harvard University Press, 2017.

Heywood, Linda M., and John K. Thornton. *Central Africans, Atlantic Creoles, and the Foundation of the Americas: Privateering, Colonial Expansion, and the African Presence in Early Anglo-Dutch Settlements.* Cambridge: Cambridge University Press, 2007.

Horn, James. *A Land as God Made It: Jamestown and the Birth of America*. New York: Basic Books, 2005.

———. *1619: Jamestown and the Forging of American Democracy.* New York: Basic Books, 2018.

Hotten, John Camden. *Original Lists of Persons of Quality: Emigrants, Religious Exiles, Political Rebels, Serving Men Sold for a Term of Years, Apprentices, Children Stolen, Maidens Pressed, and Others Who Went from Great Britain to the American Plantations, 1600–1700*. 1874; reprint, Baltimore, MD: Genealogical Publishing Company, 1986.

Ives, Vernon A., ed. *The Rich Papers: Letters from Bermuda, 1615–1646*. Toronto: Published for the Bermuda National Trust by the University of Toronto Press, 1984.

Kingsbury, Susan Myra, ed. *The Records of the Virginia Company of London. Volume 1. The Court Book, 1619–1622*. Westminster, MD: Heritage Books, 2009.

———. *The Records of the Virginia Company of London. Volume 2. The Court Book, 1622–1624*. Westminster, MD: Heritage Books, 2009.

Bibliography

————. *The Records of the Virginia Company of London.* Volume 3. *Documents I, 1607–1622.* Westminster, MD: Heritage Books, 2009.

————. *The Records of the Virginia Company of London.* Volume 4. *Miscellaneous Documents, 1606–1626.* Washington, DC: U.S. Government Printing Office, 1906–1935.

Kupperman, Karen Ordahl. *Providence Island, 1630–1641.* New York: Cambridge University Press, 1993.

Lach, Donald F., and Edwin J. Van Kley. *Asia in the Making of Europe.* Volume 3. *A Century of Advance.* Chicago: University of Chicago Press, 1998.

Lefroy, John Henry. *The History of the Bermudas or Summer Islands.* Kessinger Legacy Reprints. A History of Bermuda (MS. in the British Museum, *Sloan.*) 1609; reprinted, London: Hakluyt Society, 2010.

————. *Memorials of the Discovery and Early Settlement of the Bermudas or Somers Islands, 1515–1685 (i.e., 1511–1687).* London: Longmans, Green, and Company, 1879.

MacDonald, Edgar, and Richard Slatten. *Surry County (Virginia) Tithables, 1668–1703.* Baltimore, MD: Clearfield, 2007.

McCartney, Martha W. *Jamestown People to 1800: Landowners, Public Officials, Minorities, and Native Leaders.* Baltimore, MD: Genealogical Publishing Company, 2012.

————. *Virginia Immigrants and Adventurers, 1607–1635: A Biographical Dictionary.* Baltimore, MD: Genealogical Publishing Company, 2007.

McIlwaine, H. R., and Virginia State Library. *Minutes of the Council and General Court of Colonial Virginia, 1622–1632, 1670–1676, with Notes and Excerpts from Original Council and General Court Records, into 1683, Now Lost.* Richmond, VA: Colonial Press, 1924. https://archive.org/details/minutesofcouncil00virg.

Morris, Robert. *Women on the Farm, 1580–1660.* Bristol, UK: Stuart Press, 1999.

Morrison, E. M. *A Brief History of Isle of Wight County.* Norfolk, VA, 1907.

Neill, Edward Duffield. *Virginia Carolorum: The Colony under the Rule of Charles the First and Second.* Albany, NY: J. Munsell's & Sons, 1886.

Bibliography

———. *Virginia Company of London: Extracts from Their Manuscript Transactions: With Notes*. Washington, DC: U.S. Government Printing Office, 1868.

———. *Virginia Vetusta, during the Reign of James the First*. Albany, NY: J. Munsell's & Sons, 1885.

Nugent, Nell Marion. *Cavaliers and Pioneers: Abstracts of Virginia Land Patents and Grants 1623–1800*. Baltimore, MD: Clearfield, 2004.

Packwood, Cyril Outerbridge. *Chained on the Rock: Slavery in Bermuda*. New York: E. Torres, 1975.

Pages, Leon. *Histoire de la Religion Chretienne au Japon depuis 1598 jusqu'a 1651*. Paris: Charles Douniol, 1869.

St. George, Henry, and Richard St. George. *Visitation of London: Anno Domini 1633, 1634, and 1635. Made . . . .* Volume 17. n.p.: n.p., n.d.

Stuart, Rob. *Pigs, Goats, and Poultry, 1580–1660*. Bristol, UK: Stuart Press, 1999.

Thornton, John. *Africa and Africans in the Making of the Atlantic World, 1400–1800*. 2nd edition. Cambridge: Cambridge University Press, 1999.

———. *A Cultural History of the Atlantic World, 1250–1820*. Cambridge: Cambridge University Press, 2012.

Tyler, Lyon Gardiner, ed. *Narratives of Early Virginia, 1606–1625*. New York: Charles Scribner's Sons, 1907. https://catalog.hathitrust.org/Record/001263599.

Vivian, J. L., and Henry H. Drake, eds. *Visitation of the County of Cornwall, in the Year of 1620*. London: Harleian Society, 1874.

Walsh, Lorena S. *From Calabar to Carters Gove: The History of the Virginia Slave Community*. Charlottesville: University Press of Virginia, 1997.

———. *Motives of Honor, Pleasure, and Profit: Plantation Management in the Colonial Chesapeake, 1607–1763*. Chapel Hill: University of North Carolina Press.

Whitelaw, Ralph T. *Virginia's Eastern Shore*. 1951; reprint, Camden, ME: Picton Press, 1998.

Woodson, Isobel B., and Robert F. Woodson. *Virginia Tithables from Burned Record Counties*. Greenville, SC: Southern Historical Press, 2018.

Bibliography

Wooley, Benjamin. *Savage Kingdom: The True Story of Jamestown, 1607, and the Settlement of America.* New York: Harper Press, 2007.

Journals and Other Periodicals

Ballagh, James Curtis. "The Institutional Origin of Slavery." *Conservative Review, a Quarterly* 2 (August 1899).

Bernhard, Virginia. "Beyond the Chesapeake: The Contrasting Status of Blacks in Bermuda, 1616–1663." *Journal of Southern History* 54, no. 4 (1988): 550.

Boddie, John Bennett. "Edward Bennett of London and Virginia." *William and Mary Quarterly* 13, no. 2 (April 1933): 117–30.

Coldham, Peter Wilson. "The Voyage of the *Neptune* to Virginia, 1618–1619, and the Disposition of Its Cargo." *Virginia Magazine of History and Biography* 87, no. 1 (1979): 30–67.

Cook, Minnie G. "Frances Grevill West Piersey Mathews." *William and Mary Quarterly* 15, no. 3 (July 1935): 299–303. doi:10.2307/1923185.

Craven, Wesley Frank. "The Earl of Warwick, a Speculator in Piracy." *Hispanic American Historical Review* 10, no. 4 (1930): 457–79.

———. "An Introduction to the History of Bermuda." *William and Mary Quarterly*, 2nd series, 17, nos. 2, 3, 4; 18, no. 1 (1937–1938).

Donoghue, John. "'Out of the Land of Bondage': The English Revolution and the Atlantic Origins of Abolition." *American Historical Review* 115, no. 4 (October 2010): 943–74. https://doi.org/10.1086/ahr.115.4.943.

Hashaw, Tim. "Malungu: The African Origin of American Melungeons." *Eclectica* (July/August 2001). http://www.eclectica.org.

Hecht, Irene. "The Virginia Muster of 1624/5 as a Source for Demographic History." *William and Mary Quarterly*, 3rd series, 30, no. 1 (January 1973): 65–92.

Maruko, Mani. "Spanish Envoy Celebrates 400-Year Relationship." *Japan Times,* October 7, 2013. www.japantimes.co.jp.

Mathes, W. Michael. "A Quarter Century of Trans-Pacific Diplomacy: New Spain and Japan, 1592–1617." *Journal of Asian History* 24, no. 1 (1990): 1–29. http://www.jstor.org/stable/41925377.

Bibliography

"Minutes of the Council and General Court, 1622–1624." *Virginia Magazine of History and Biography* 19, no. 2 (1911): 113–48. http://www.jstor.org/stable/4243124.

"Minutes of the Council and General Court, 1622–1629 (Continued)." *Virginia Magazine of History and Biography* 23, no. 1 (1915): 1–23. http://www.jstor.org/stable/4243402.

Neill, Edward D., and Nathaniel Butler. "Virginia Carolorum: The Colony during the Days of Charles the First and Second." *Pennsylvania Magazine of History and Biography* 9, no. 2 (1885): 134–66.

Quisenberry, A. C. "The First Pioneer Families of Virginia." *Register of Kentucky State Historical Society* 11, no. 32 (1913): 55-77. http://www.jstor.org/stable/23367151.

"Randolph Manuscript, The: Virginia Seventeenth Century Records (Continued)." *Virginia Magazine of History and Biography* 17, no. 3 (July 1909): 225–48. https://www.jstor.org/stable/4242990?seq=1#metadata_info_tab_contents.

Robinson, Conway. "Virginia Council and General Court Records, 1640–1641." *Virginia Magazine of History and Biography* 11, no. 3 (1904): 277–84. http://www.jstor.org/stable/4242616.

Sluiter, Engel. "New Light on the '20 and Odd Negroes' Arriving in Virginia, August 1619." *William and Mary Quarterly,* 3rd series, 54 (1997): 396–98.

Surry County Court Records. *Magazine of Virginia Genealogy* 22–24, various issues.

"Surry County Tithables, 1698, 1699, 1700." *Virginia Genealogical Society Quarterly* 24, no. 2 (May 1986).

"Surry County Tithables, 1701, 1702, 1703." *Virginia Genealogical Society Quarterly* 24, no. 3 (August 1986).

Thorndale, William. "The Virginia Census of 1619/20." *Magazine of Virginia Genealogy* 33, no. 3 (Summer 1995): 155–70.

Thornton, John. "The African Experience of the 20 and Odd Negroes Arriving in Virginia in 1619." *William and Mary Quarterly*, 3rd series, 55, no. 3 (July 1998): 421–34. https://www.jstor.org/stable/2674531.

Turman, Nora Miller, and Mark C. Lewis. "The Will of Ann Littleton of Northampton County, Virginia, 1656." *Virginia Magazine of*

History and Biography 75, no. 1 (1967): 11–21. http://www.jstor.org/stable/4247277.

Virginia Historical Society. "Virginia in 1635: The Deposing of Governor Harvey." *Virginia Magazine of History and Biography* 8, no. 3 (January 1901): 299–306. https://www.jstor.org/stable/4242360.

Virginia Magazine of History and Biography 1. Philip Alexander Bruce and William Glover (eds.), Virginia Historical Society (January 1893).

"Virginia in 1626–27." *Virginia Magazine of History and Biography* 16, no. 1 (1908): 30–38.

Wolfe, Brendan. "William Peirce (d. btw. 1645 and 1647)." Encyclopedia Virginia. Virginia Humanities. https://www.encyclopediavirginia.org/Peirce_William_d_btw_1645_and_1647.

Museums and Exhibits

San Juan Bautista Museum, Ishinomaki, Japan.

Sendai (Japan) City Museum, *Records of the Date House, Keichō-Genna*, 1995.

———. *The World and Japan: Tensho and Keicho Missions to Europe, 16th–17th Century,* 1995.

Websites

The Ancient Wilsford Family of Devonshire, and Their Later Jamestown, James City County, Virginia Colony. http://www.geocities.ws/madelinefelkins/WillifordWilford.htm.

Behrens/Tucker Ancestors. https://wc.rootsweb.com/cgi-bin/igm.cgi?op=GET&db=bradsdata&id=I11433.

The Charter of New England—1620. http://avalon.law.yale.edu/17th_century/mass01.asp.

Free African Americans of Virginia, North Carolina, South Carolina, Maryland and Delaware. http://www.freeafricanamericans.com/.

Goyen Family 2000–12 Dec Newsletter. https://goyengoinggowengoyneandgone.com/2000-12-dec-newsletter-grf/.

The Living and Dead in Virginia, February 16, 1623. USGenWeb Archives. http://files.usgwarchives.net/va/jamestown/census/1623censl.txt.

Bibliography

"Marmaduke Rayner." http://www.carolana.com/Carolina/Explorers/marmadukerayner.html.

Materials Related to the Keicho-Era Mission in Europe (Japan and Spain). UNESCO Memory of the World, 2012. htttp://www.unesco.org/new/fileadmin/MULTIMEDIA/HQ/CI/CI/pdf/mow/nomination_forms/Japan_Spain_keicho.pdf.

McCartney, Martha W. "A Study of Virginia Indians and Jamestown: The First Century." Chapter 4, "Narrative History." National Park Service. https://www.nps.gov/parkhistory/online_books/jame1/moretti-langholtz/chap4.htm.

———. "Virginia's First Africans." Virginia Humanities. https://www.encyclopediavirginia.org/virginia_s_first_africans#start_entry.

"Nathaniel Basse of London and Jamestown." https://www.scribd.com/document/257650518/Nathaniel-Basse-of-London-and-Jamestown.

Pilgrim Ship Lists. https://www.packrat.pro.com/ships/shiplist.htm.

"Slavery and the Law in Virginia." Colonial Williamsburg. https://www.history.org/history/teaching/slavelaw.cfm.

Swift, M. "The Imbangala: Death and War Culture." Black Then: Discovering Our History. October 12, 2017. https://blackthen.com/imbangala-death-war-culture/.

"Temperance Flowerdew." Liberty Letters. Filing Cabinet, 2006. http://www.libertyletters.com/resources/jamestown/temperance-flowerdew.php.

Virginia Laws of Servitude and Slavery (1643–1691). http://www.indiana.edu/~kdhist/H105-documents-web/week03/VAlaws1643.html.

Voyages: The Trans-Atlantic Slave Trade Database. Emory University et al. http://slavevoyages.org/voyage.

Index

Numbers in *italics* indicate figures and tables. Names in *italics* indicate ships.

Index

Index

Index

Index

Index

Index

Index

Index

triracial community in, 145

Virginia Company of London, 34, 37
   Bennett and, 50
   financial condition of, xii–xiii
   Gondomar accusing of piracy, 95
   investigating *Bautista* piracy,
     18–19
   political infighting in, xi, xiii, 15,
     39, 42, 96, 118
   rules and laws of, 95
   Sandys as treasurer of, 38 (*See also*
     Sandys, Edwin)
   Warwick withdrawing from, 15

Virginia Council, 15

Walde family, 146

Walker, John, 131

Warrasquarake (a Bennett plantation),
   50–51, 56n35, 109

Warwick, 13, 108

Warwick (Second Earl of Warwick).
   See Rich, Robert

Waterson, John, 115

Webb, Daniel, 133

West, Francis, 41, 53, 67, *68*, 78, 79,
   123

West, John, 53

West, Thomas, xii, xiii, 35, 53

West & Shirley Plantation, 62

Weyanoke, 45

Wharton family, 146

White, Francis, 77

White Lion, 120, 121, 122, 124, 129,
   132, 147n30

Africans placed on, from *San Juan
   Bautista*, 59–60
   arriving in Virginia, 7–8, 43, 46,
     107
   in Bermuda, 7, 72, 74
   denied entry to Bermuda, 49, 107
   seizing the *San Juan Bautista*,
     6–7
   travels of, 9, 43, *104–5*

Wilford, Cecily, 37

Wilkins family, 146

William (African at Flowerdew), 45,
   67, 76, 109

Wilson family, 146

Windmill Point, 45

Woodson, John, 43–44, 47, 109

Woodson, Robert, 42

Woodson, Sarah, 42, 43–44, 47, 109

Wray, Frances, 37

Wyatt, Francis, 48, 110, 132

Yeardley, Argall, 42, 52

Yeardley, Elizabeth, 42

Yeardley, Francis, 43

Yeardley, George, xii, xiv, 8, 33, 38,
     41–45, 47, 109, George, 122
   Africans with, 59, 66, 68, 82–86
   involvement of, in piracy episode,
     42–43
   meeting with Jope, 43
   trading for Africans, 43
   as Virginia's largest landowner, 42

Yeardley, Temperance Flowerdew, 42,
   43, 47, 110

About the Author

Kathryn Knight, who uses the pen name K. I. Knight, is an international award–winning author, genealogist, historian, public speaker, cemetery preservationist, and land development consultant. Over the last twelve years, Knight has logged over twenty thousand hours researching the first documented Africans to arrive in the English settlement of Virginia in 1619. In 2016, as an advisory board member for Project 1619, she cocurated the "1619 First African Landing" exhibit at the Hampton History Museum in Hampton, Virginia.

Her passion is unrivaled and strongly evident in her published writings. Her literary work includes the Fate & Freedom series—a five-star / gold-medal-winning historical trilogy detailing the lives of the 1619 Africans—as well as her nonfiction work, *Unveiled: The Twenty & Odd.*

Knight's adventure began in 2006 when she discovered that her husband knew very little about his ancestry. For Christmas 2006 she gave her husband's family an ancestral chart from the present day back to the early 1600s, when the Knights resided in the early settlement of Virginia. With excitement, her father-in-law made a small request. He recalled an early childhood memory of a woman he would see on occasion while visiting at his grandmother's house. He remembered her dark skin and possibly her last name, Sweat. After substantial research, Knight found the mysterious woman to be a Sweat cousin.

Knight's curiosity about her husband's Sweat line led her back to the 1640s, where documentation showed how and when the line originated. An order for punishment was issued involving Robert Sweat, an Englishman, and an African woman, charged with fornication. The African woman would prove to be Margaret Cornish, one of the first Africans in the English settlement of Virginia. Knight's curiosity turned into an uncontrollable passion to resolve her many unanswered questions about the Africans who arrived in Virginia in 1619.

In 2011 Knight commissioned a painting by the highly acclaimed maritime artist Richard C. Moore titled *The Battle of the* San Juan Bautista. Her passion quickly turned to an addiction; she decided that she must find the true story behind their arrival, where they came from, and who they were. After using cluster genealogy tactics, Knight discovered a different narrative than that delivered by historical societies and classrooms. Family associations and connections were revealed, and political allies aligned as Knight became engrossed in every documented aspect of their lives. With her new research and documentation telling a truer story of the 1619 Africans, Knight decided she had to share the facts with the world.

Knight is the secretary of the board of directors of the Florida Authors & Publishers Association. She is a member of the National Genealogy Society, the Afro American Historical and

Genealogical Society, the Florida State Genealogy Society, the Virginia Genealogy Society, the Virginia Historical Society, the Florida Historical Society, the American Historical Association, the Genealogy Speakers Guild, the Association of Professional Genealogists, the Alliance of Independent Authors, the National Association of Professional Women, and the director of 1619 Genealogy. The mother of three adult children, Knight lives in Central Florida with her husband, Tom.

In addition to UNVEILED – *The Twenty & Odd*, Knight has written the international award winning series Fate & Freedom. Fate & Freedom brings to life the first Africans to land in England's America in the years of 1619–1620 as you experience the paths they walked on their great journey to freedom.

Fate & Freedom Book I – *The Middle Passage*

Fate & Freedom Book II – *The Turning Tides*

Fate & Freedom Book III – *On Troubled Shores*

Fate & Freedom – *Research Companion* (Coming Soon)

The *Research Companion* will include additional historical and genealogical research about those who descend from the first Africans, bringing some ancestral lines to the current day.

Hope you will join the journey!

First Freedom Publishing

FATE & FREEDOM

RESEARCH COMPANION

K. I. KNIGHT

CPSIA information can be obtained
at www.ICGtesting.com
Printed in the USA
FFHW021646260419
52068688-57452FF